Original title:
The Warmth of Christmas Memories

Copyright © 2024 Creative Arts Management OÜ
All rights reserved.

Author: Kieran Blackwood
ISBN HARDBACK: 978-9916-94-062-4
ISBN PAPERBACK: 978-9916-94-063-1

Scribbled Wishes in the Snow

Snowflakes dancing on my nose,
I build a snowman, with big blue toes.
He wobbles and flops with a grin so wide,
Yet down he goes for a slippery slide.

Hot cocoa spills on my winter socks,
I slip on ice while walking, oh what a shock!
Laughter echoes as I tumble right,
Guess I'll stick to the warmth inside tonight!

Voices of Winter's Embrace

Carolers sing off-key by the tree,
Their voices crack like a festive decree.
Santa's sleigh got stuck in the snow,
He's shouting, 'More reindeer, let's make it go!'

Grandma's cookies are lopsided and burnt,
Yet every bite, my taste buds are spurned.
We munch and we laugh, oh what a scene,
Celebrating flavors that defy the routine!

Cradles of Childhood Cheer

Racing down the hallway, my socks a blur,
I trip and I tumble, but what's the deter?
Presents are hiding, oh where can they be?
I'll dive in the pile, just wait and see!

A game with the cat, he swats at the bow,
It's a questionable gift, but what does he know?
Amidst all the chaos and playful delight,
These shenanigans sparkle, so merry and bright!

A Tapestry of Twinkling Lights

Twinkling bulbs flash in a dazzle so loud,
I trip on the cord, what a clumsy proud!
The tree stands tall, but lopsided for sure,
O Christmas, you silly, who knew you'd allure?

Rudolph's nose blinks like a disco ball,
While Uncle Bob dances, we all start to fall.
Jingle bells ringing, and laughter ignites,
This festive fiasco is pure holiday sights!

Time-Honored Traditions

Grandma's fruitcake, dense as a brick,
We all took a bite, it made us all sick.
Uncle Joe snores loud, like a grizzly bear,
Only to wake up, with frosting in hair.

Tree covered in tinsel, a glittery mess,
We'd blame the cat when it's time to confess.
Ornaments tangled, like lights in a knot,
Dad says, "It's fine, just takes a good shot!"

Notes of Nostalgia

Singing off-key to carols so bright,
Then tripping on boots, that gave us a fright.
Pine-scented air mixed with mom's hot stew,
Made us all giggle like the joy was brand new.

Wrapping up gifts that were slightly too late,
Last year's presents? Well, they still look great!
We'd joke and we'd laugh, with our hearts full of cheer,
Unwrapping each one, like it's just disappeared.

Yesterday's Laughter

Santa got stuck in the flue, what a sight,
We pulled him out, but he gave us a fright.
With cookies all crumbled, and milk spilled about,
We laughed till our bellies were round as a bout.

Snowball fights turned into snow-tastrophes,
Sledding downhill was a total mischief.
One tumble and roll, we'd all hit the slush,
Laughter erupted, in the frosty rush.

Cloaked in Comfort

Grandpa's old sweater, three sizes too large,
He wore it with pride like he's leading a charge.
Hot cocoa spills and marshmallows afloat,
A funny mix-up like the Christmas we wrote.

Midnight snacks claimed by a sneaky raccoon,
We found him munching beneath the full moon.
Laughter erupted, as he made his escape,
With a cocoa mustache, and a sweet little shape.

Memories Wrapped in Ribbons

A box of lights with tangled strings,
A cat naps soundly, dreaming of things.
Mom's slippers go flying, it's quite the show,
As Uncle Joe dances, despite the snow.

Grandma's old eggnog sits on the shelf,
With a hint of spice, it confuses itself.
Cousins all giggle at the fruitcake surprise,
While a snowman outside wears dad's old ties.

Socks that don't match, oh what a sight,
We toast with hot cocoa, the mood feels just right.
Tickles and laughter, all around the room,
As we cherish these times, let the silly bloom.

Toasts to Togetherness

We raise our mugs in a joyful cheer,
Grandpa starts teasing, we always want to hear.
A toast for each cousin, and one for the dog,
Who's hiding their treats under the old fog.

The roast's gone rogue, on the floor it's found,
Oh, what a family! Just sit back, astound.
Silly stories are shared as we dig right in,
With Auntie's last mishap and Uncle's old grin.

Laughter erupts at the silliest tales,
Of snowball fights ending with snow-covered veils.
Cookies baked badly, but smiles remain,
Hands raised together, through joy and through pain.

Snowflake Stories

Outside it is snowing, a magical scene,
While inside we're busy with cookies and cream.
Sledding adventures, a face full of snow,
Caught on the camera, so funny to show.

Cousins are twirling, a conga-line spree,
And someone gets tangled, oh what a sight to see!
Frosty's a legend, but he drifts with the wind,
And dad learned to snowboard, now that's how it's pinned.

Among all the giggles, a story is told,
Of snowball wars fought brave, valiant, and bold.
With gifts by the fireside, both big and small,
We have our tales mixed with laughter and all.

Warm Winks of Winter

The fireplace crackles, with magical sparks,
As Grandma swoops in, yelling, "Who's stole the tarts?"
A wink and a smile from each little face,
Holding a secret, in this warm winter space.

The kids are all dressed like giant marshmallows,
Sleds flying fast while the laughter just bellows.
Mom trips on the carpet, and down goes her drink,
We all burst with giggles, hey, what do you think?

Pine needles scatter, as we deck out the tree,
In ornaments silly, matching none of we.
With cocoa in hand, that's where joy combines,
And every sweet moment like glitter just shines.

A Melody of Memories

Jingle bells clatter, a cat takes a seat,
Stuck on the tree, oh what a feat!
Granddad's still singing his off-key tune,
While grandma's lost track of the nice and the rude.

Mittens piled high, a snowball fight,
Uncle Joe's aim was not quite right.
The snowman looks worried, his hat's a bit crooked,
As we sip hot cocoa and munch on the cookied.

Coziness and Cheer

Socks on the fire, what a great place,
They're popping and cracking, we make a race.
The lights are all blinking, the dog's in a loop,
Chasing his tail, oh what a goof troop!

Ribbons of laughter, so bright in the air,
Dad trips on the garland, oh no, it's a scare!
A pie in the oven, who should we blame?
Mom said she'd bake it, it's not the same!

Emblazed in Laughter

Each gift a surprise, the wrapping is bright,
A present for me? Oh, what a delight!
But wait, it's just socks with a glittery view,
The gift that keeps giving, from Aunt Sue, it's true!

Cookies for Santa, or so I thought,
But Rudolph just ate them, now I'm left fraught.
No milk in the fridge, a glass of old tea,
This Christmas may just end in a comedy spree!

Solstice Serenades

Carols are ringing, off-key but loud,
The neighbors all laugh, they're quite the crowd.
Harold's dance moves, a little bizarre,
He'll surely be famous, in a weird way, so far!

Eggnog spills over, our favorite drink,
It could double as glue, oh what do you think?
Laughter erupts, the magic is clear,
This silly old gathering is one we hold dear.

A Warmth That Lingers

In socks mismatched, we dance with glee,
The lights that twinkle, a sight to see.
Grandma's fruitcake, oh what a treat,
Even the cat says, "This can't be beat!"

We sip hot cocoa, marshmallow fluff,
Mom's telling stories, though we've heard enough.
The dog steals a roll, to our surprise,
As we all burst out laughing, tears in our eyes.

Gathering Around the Glowing Hearth

Gathered close, with blankets thick,
Uncle Joe starts his magic trick.
With a hat and a rabbit, he's lost his mind,
The rabbit hops off — no one can find!

The fire crackles, sparks fly high,
We roast marshmallows, oh me, oh my!
S'mores are devoured, sticky and sweet,
As Dad yells, "Fire!" — it's just our feet!

Chasing Shadows of Festive Echoes

Snowmen stand tall, with smiles so wide,
But one got a pumpkin, what a bizarre ride!
Carrot noses, eyes of coal,
In the yard, a Santa with a roll!

We chase shadows, giggling, carefree,
The neighbors peek out, oh, who could it be?
It's just us kids, a mischief-filled crew,
With reindeer antics, and a sled that flew!

Gifts of Time Tied with Ribbons

With ribbon untied, the chaos begins,
We're all on a hunt — who wins?
A box labeled "Yarn" contains a rat,
A gift from Aunt Sue — no one saw that!

We unwrap the laughter, layer by layer,
Each present a puzzle, let's be a player.
As paper flies, it's a joyful mess,
A Christmas so weird, who could guess less?

Unraveled Gifts

The ribbons flew like birds in flight,
Hiding snacks, oh what a sight!
Wrapped so tight, the paper screamed,
Hope you like what I dreamed!

A box of socks, a rubber duck,
Thought I'd fill it with my luck!
I gave you sweets, you gave me chills,
With every bite, we got our thrills!

Portraits of Peace

In sweaters bright, we pose and grin,
Next year, let's aim for the win!
Dad's beard caught in the cookie jar,
Merry chaos, it's our bizarre!

A picture taken, faces misaligned,
Mom's hairdo—what a find!
Capture the night with spicy cheer,
Snapshot of laughter through the year!

Savoring Sweet Moments

Cookies stacked like towers high,
Oops! One fell, oh my, oh my!
Milk spilled like magic tricks,
Giggling kids with sticky licks!

A feast begins, but wait, what's this?
The cat stole pie, it's such pure bliss!
We laugh and munch on all that's here,
Sweet moments like this, oh dear!

Childhood Echoes

The snowballs fly, oh how they flew,
Remember when we hit Aunt Sue?
Laughter ringing in the snowy air,
As frosty flakes tangled in our hair!

With sleds that tipped and cheeks so red,
We'd race till we crashed and fell, instead!
Those echoes of giggles, a fantasy,
Hold them close, they're pure jubilee!

Snowy Embraces

Snowflakes dance like crazy crowds,
While we chase them like little kids,
With snowmen dressed in mismatched clothes,
And carrots that forget where they hid.

Hot cocoa spills on my brand new coat,
As marshmallows float like fluffy dreams,
Uncle Joe slipped on the icy path,
And fell right into mom's yarn schemes.

We sing off-key, it's a joyous sound,
Mistletoe hangs above our heads,
Nan's cookies are as hard as bricks,
Yet we eat them all, just like she said.

Amid the laughter and goofy brawls,
We cherish moments, though some are loud,
Each snowy hug and silly fall,
Leaves a smile that's winter proud.

Treasures of the Heart

A gift that's wrapped with sparkly tape,
Looks fancy but holds a plastic toy,
Granddad chuckles at our surprise,
"Best secret ever!" says our boy.

The cat leaps up, oh what a mess,
With ribbons wrapped 'round her tiny paws,
She thinks it's all a game to play,
While we shout and give her applause.

A fruitcake sits, a family curse,
With layers that could stop a car,
Yet every year, we slice a piece,
Making legends of our bizarre.

The stories shared around the tree,
Are treasures that fill our hearts with cheer,
With laughter echoing through the night,
We gather close, year after year.

Yule Legends Revisited

The elf on the shelf, he's up to tricks,
He dances on the TV with glee,
While we're convinced that he's watching us,
Is he a spy or just goofy?

Stockings stuffed with socks and sweets,
Mom's got an eye for crafty seams,
Dad forgets to take a hint,
When asked to fix those broken dreams.

We gather 'round with lights aglow,
As Grandpa nods off in his chair,
Then wakes with tales from long ago,
Of Christmas magic that fills the air.

Each legend fills our hearts with joy,
As we swap tales and share more laughs,
With each new tale, our spirits soar,
Brother takes charge of the silly crafts.

Frost-Kissed Hues

The tree is crooked—it leans to one side,
With tinsel that looks like a bird's nest,
Ornaments swinging in a wild ride,
While the angel on top gets no rest.

Chilly winds whistle through the streets,
As we try to build a snow fort high,
But all we create is a slushy mess,
Guess the snowball fight is worth a try.

Grandma's sweater is two sizes too big,
In colors that clash like a wild dream,
She loves it still—the warmth it brings,
While we try not to giggle and scream.

With mischief brewing, the night takes flight,
As we recount tales with twinkling eyes,
In these frosty hues filled with laughter,
Are the lovely moments, our greatest prize.

Mistletoe Moments

Under the mistletoe, I made my move,
Tripped on my feet, what a funny groove!
Kissed a dear aunt who wore red lipstick,
Now I sport a print that's quite the trick.

Grandpa told jokes, oh, how they did soar,
Laughed until we fell, rolling on the floor!
A cat stole the scene, with a Christmas bow,
Lurking by the snack—oh, what a show!

A Gathering of Hearts

Family around, with stories to share,
Uncle Sam's tales, a wild, wacky flair!
Sister's new dance looks like a spastic move,
We laugh till we cry, can't help but approve.

Cousins all gathered, a photo we take,
But one of us blinked—watch that funny face break!
Gifts wrapped in layers, with endless tape,
Now we're stuck in a paper-slicing escape!

Gingerbread Dreams

Baked a gingerbread house, it leaned to the side,
The roof caved in, surprised we all cried!
I took a big bite, frosting on my nose,
Santa's not the only one with the joy that he shows.

Cookies went missing, who could it be?
The dog gave a glance, as guilty as can be!
Sprinkles on his snout, icing in his fur,
Is this canine a chef? Oh, what a stir!

Cocoa and Comfort

Cocoa in hand, I warmed up my soul,
But spilled it on Grandma, oh, how I roll!
She laughed so hard, the mug in her grip,
Now she's the one with hot chocolate on her lip.

Marshmallows floating, kids on the floor,
Bouncing around like never before!
A blanket fort made, it's cozy and bright,
But where's the cocoa? Oh, what a sight!

Sledding Down Memory Lane

Snowy hills were our playground,
We raced with laughter, face full of cold.
Sleds that flew like parachutes,
Landing in piles, stories untold.

Hot cocoa spills on mom's new chair,
Marshmallow fights, giggles and cheer.
We dressed like penguins, layers galore,
With hats so big, we could barely steer.

Mittens soaked from snowball wars,
Friction burns from sledding too fast.
But who needs warmth when you've got friends,
To laugh through chilly moments amassed.

Days like these, tangled in glee,
Noses pink under twinkling lights.
Who knew sledding could feel so grand,
With memories stored in snowy heights.

Fond Embraces Wrapped in Brightness

Auntie's hugs, like marshmallows puffed,
Squeeze too tight, you can't escape.
Her perfume smells like peppermint dreams,
Wrapped up tightly, escaping the drape.

Christmas lights blink in rhythm divine,
We twirled under stars from the attic.
Grandma's cookies, burnt just a tad,
But love made all the flavors ecstatic.

Uncle Joe's dance, such a sight!
Two left feet, but he owns the floor.
His reindeer antlers fall to the ground,
Making our sides split, hearts wanting more.

In the chaos, we find our peace,
Mom's laughter floats, joyous and bright.
Wrapped in hugs, and banter so sweet,
Family felt like magic that night.

Holly and Hope in Gentle Hues

Bright ribbons wrapped around laughter,
Holly hung asking for a kiss.
Grandpa reads with a twinkle, how sweet,
Stories that promise a little bliss.

Wrapping paper, a shimmery mess,
Cats dive in with no ounce of shame.
Presents tossed like snowflakes adrift,
Who needs toys when the cat's the game?

Ballet slippers dance with delight,
A tree decorated with eco-style.
Out of the box, our dreams take flight,
We leap and spin, all dressed with a smile.

Memories twinkle like ornaments hung,
In every crackle, a chuckle hides.
While holly and color bring us together,
It's the quirks that make our joy wide.

Echoing Laughter Through Frosted Windows

Frosted panes show our antics bold,
Snowmen with noses, shriveled and small.
We posed for pictures, stuck out our tongues,
Hoping the snow wouldn't end in a brawl.

Outside the world froze in silent bliss,
While inside we ate all the treats.
Nibbled on cookies, frosting on noses,
Racing each other for seconds and feats.

Muffin disasters, flour in the air,
Mom's face a mix of love and dismay.
Fire crackles, bringing warmth so tight,
Who needs a recipe? We play! We play!

Laughter echoes through frosted frames,
Each giggle a gift, fresh and bright.
Time stands still, in this cheerful realm,
Where memories glow like the stars at night.

Family Ties and Twinkling Lights

Gather round the fabled tree,
Where chaos swirls, oh can't you see?
Uncle Joe brings "holiday cheer,"
With laughter spilling in his beer.

Aunt May's fruitcake, hard as stone,
Leaves everyone to groan and moan.
But in the corner, kids conspire,
To set the cat's tail on fire!

The lights are dim, the bulbs are bright,
Grandpa's snoring, what a sight!
While stories told take odd twists,
And we all ponder, 'Did we exist?'

Gathered close with warmth inside,
Swapped old tales we cannot hide.
As magic swirls in silly flights,
These moments glow like twinkling lights.

Keeping Christmas Close

Sneaky Santa, what a tale,
Wrapped in jokes that never fail.
Our secret stash of tasty treats,
I see you nibbling on the sweets!

With mismatched socks, we all parade,
Into the living room, unafraid.
Grandma's punch, all spicy and nice,
A potent brew; we pay the price!

The tree is wobbling side to side,
Each ornament's a sloshed ride.
As laughter dances through the air,
I swear I saw a flying chair!

With goofy hats and silly songs,
We've turned it up; we can't go wrong.
In every hug, a quirky boast,
This time of year, we love the most.

Remnants of Yuletide Joy

Beneath the lights, we gather round,
As old tunes play, a timeless sound,
And Grandma's knitted hats, mismatched,
Are what our joyous hearts have hatched.

The cookies burned, a crispy fate,
Yet still we laugh and contemplate.
Uncle Fred tried to gift us all,
A singing fish, it made us fall!

With grand tales told of Christmas past,
We share the giggles, make them last,
As secrets spill from mouths agape,
Like Grandpa's antics, what a shape!

Through all the love, and laughter's grace,
These silly moments, we embrace.
In every glimmer, laughter's near,
Our hearts ring loud with festive cheer!

Ancestral Cheer

With cousin cards that all are wrong,
We sit back, laughing all night long.
A feast so grand, who could survive?
There's turkey leg and pie, oh my!

A game of charades turns to mayhem,
As Auntie shrieks, "You'll never tame him!"
Dressed up as elves, we laugh and play,
Our family shenanigans on display.

Uncle's jokes, they never end,
As every punchline twists a bend.
With eggnog spills and jolly roars,
We keep returning for more and more.

In cozy hugs, our hearts expand,
Through silly stories, hand in hand.
With love and laughter, it is clear,
This is the season we all hold dear.

Milestones in Mirth

A cat in a hat, what a sight,
Chasing paper balls, oh what delight!
Grandma slipped on the ice with grace,
Now she's the star of our family space.

Uncle Bob's dance, quite the show,
Spilled his drink all over Joe.
We laughed until our sides would ache,
A Christmas to remember, make no mistake!

The turkey's burnt, but we don't care,
We gobble up cookies, in our chairs,
A battle of snowballs, who'll take the prize?
Laughter erupts as the snow monster lies.

With tinsel hair and a jingle bell,
We've spun around like a carousel.
In moments like these, love fills the air,
Memories knitted, beyond compare.

Silhouettes of Celebration

Tinsel stuck on the dog's tail,
He runs like the wind, a furry snail.
A mishap with lighting, oh what a scene,
We lit up the house like a bad Halloween!

Grandpa's snoring under the tree,
With a cookie stash, as happy as can be.
Sister sings off-key, what a cheer,
We hand her a mic, she's the star here!

Reindeer games that went awry,
A flying sleigh ride, nearly to the sky.
We laughed 'til we cried, can't keep track,
Of who wore the antlers, and who wore the sack.

In the warmth of the room, jokes fly around,
Echoes of laughter, the best kind of sound.
We celebrate quirks that make us whole,
In each silly moment, love's the goal.

Threads of Togetherness

Knitting sweaters far too tight,
We all look like sausages tonight!
A cheer when the cookies somehow flop,
"Let's order pizza!" — Oh, what a swap!

Grandma's putting marshmallows in stew,
We debate if that's something we'd do.
A game of charades, hilariously poor,
We act like penguins, and then roll on the floor!

In a mix of laughter, joy floods the night,
With inside jokes that feel just right.
A gift from last year, still in the wrap,
"Is this my old sweater?" it's all a trap!

With friends and family, we gather close,
Counting the blessings that matter most.
In funny mishaps, we find our cheer,
In the love we share, we hold most dear.

Whispers in the Wind

A snowman fell and rolled away,
Chasing after him was quite the play.
Our snowflakes' battle, a frosty war,
And hot cocoa spills on the kitchen floor!

There's a sock on the cat — what a funny sight,
As he struts through the room, all filled with delight.
Dad's got candy canes stuck in his beard,
"It's all part of Christmas," he proudly cheered!

Slippers on the dog, he's a merry sight,
Barking at bells that jingle all night.
We tell silly stories, and laugh 'til we cry,
As the moon shines bright in the frosty sky.

Around the table, our hearts are aglow,
With tales of mishaps in the recent snow.
Each chuckle, each grin, a gift that we lend,
In the spirit of joy, our hearts never end.

Echoes Beneath the Stars

Twinkling lights and silly hats,
We danced with dogs and sang with cats.
Grandma's fruitcake, a brick in disguise,
We laughed so hard, tears filled our eyes.

The sleigh ride went off a tiny cliff,
Santa yelled, 'Hey, where's my gift?'
Mistletoe hung way too high,
We all got stuck, oh my, oh my!

Frosty melted, oh what a shame,
He slipped on ice while playing a game.
We built him back with half a grin,
He winked at us, let the fun begin!

In memory's vault, joy holds the key,
Each goofy mishap, a gem, you see.
Under the stars, we raise a cheer,
For laughter shared, the best time of year!

The Hearthstone Haven

Gathered 'round the fire's glow,
Uncle Joe lost track of his toe.
He wore a sock that looked like this:
A reindeer's face, we couldn't miss!

Cookies vanished in a blink,
Elves must've come, we start to think.
Dad filled his eggnog, oh so bold,
Now he's dancing like he's five years old.

Watching the cat chase tinsel strings,
He thought he'd caught all the shiny things.
With each pounce and jump, our hearts would race,
Turns out he just wanted a cozy place.

The warmth of laughter fills the room,
As stories swirl like a fragrant plume.
Around the hearth, we share a grin,
Thanking fortune for the joyful din.

Flickering Firelight

In firelight's glow, the stories blend,
Of turkey mishaps and a sock that bend.
Mom's soufflé soared up to its height,
Then dropped like it lost its will to fight.

Cousin Larry in a Santa suit,
He couldn't fit through the front, oh, shoot!
We had a laugh, he wriggled away,
With sparkly lights, signs of dismay.

Hiding gifts became a grand old time,
I found a sweater that looked like a crime.
Neighbors peeked in with a curious glare,
'What's with that outfit? Just don't compare!'

Through flickering flames, memories rise,
With silly tales and starry skies.
We gather tight, our hearts in tune,
Creating magic beneath the moon.

Branches of the Past

Decking the halls with mismatched flair,
Some ornaments hung with delicate care.
Yet a cat played hide-and-seek in the tree,
Somersaults down — oh, what a spree!

The gifts were wrapped with duct tape woes,
Dad couldn't find where the ribbon goes.
A gingerbread house made of pure delight,
But someone nibbled it, oh, what a sight!

Forgotten socks in the Santa sack,
A mystery box we just can't keep track.
Labels askew, names in a spin,
We've learned by now, chaos must win.

Branching through laughter, we reminisce,
Each goofy moment, a hug we don't miss.
In every cheer that echoes near,
We hold those quirks so dear, so dear.

Stories Spun by the Fire's Glare

The fire crackles, stories swirl,
Uncle Joe's tales give our heads a whirl.
A cat leaps, knocking down the snacks,
Laughter erupts, despite the cracks.

Aunt Sally's sweater, oh what a sight,
Knitting gone wild, it's a true delight.
She claims it's fashion, we can't ignore,
It looks like a monster walked through the door.

A game of charades, a holiday gaffe,
Dad's dance moves make everyone laugh.
With each wild gesture, the room starts to cheer,
Even the Grinch would shed a tear.

As snowflakes drift and lights start to glow,
We cherish these moments; we love them so!
Gathered together, our hearts all align,
In this cozy chaos, everything's fine.

Joyful Reflections in Each Ornament

Each ornament hangs with a laugh and a tale,
That one's a winner, the rest seem to fail.
We reminisce over each clumsy craft,
When Grandma's glue turned joy into draft.

Remember the reindeer that fell off the tree?
Timmy's wild leap; oh, what a spree!
With mismatched socks and tinsel in hair,
Our holiday spirit can't help but flare.

We toast with cocoa, mugs all a-clink,
The dog steals a cookie; oh, what do you think?
A trial and error with laughter so bright,
As we tell stories through each sparkling light.

Memories linger, wrapped tight around,
In this jolly mess, we have truly found,
Christmas is more than the perfect display,
It's the goofy moments that make our day.

Winter's Embrace on Tender Hearts

Snowflakes stage a soft ballet,
While we haggle over which game to play.
Mom's stuffing burns, but don't let it go,
Dad's secret recipe was just for show.

Through frosty windows, children will cheer,
Snowball fights start, we'll conquer our fear.
Bitterly cold, yet kinship so sweet,
Until the snow is stuck to our feet!

Our mismatched mittens, a colorful flop,
As we stumble and giggle, we can't seem to stop.
Grandpa's old stories make time disappear,
They're funny, though half of them we might fear.

So gather around, let's craft joyful cheer,
With laughter our treasure, we hold so dear.
Through silly antics and warmth from the heart,
Every moment we share is a true work of art.

Singing Carols of Long Ago

Singing carols off-key, what a delight,
Our "angels" are more like a curious sight.
With mismatched hats and old flannel wear,
We make quite the duo—truly unaware.

Remember the time, we sang on the street?
The mailman joined in, it was quite a feat!
A cat stole the show, with a leap and a flip,
Our musical magic was soon on a trip.

As we laugh and we sing 'bout the trees and the snow,
A burst of nostalgia for days long ago.
Chilly fingers wrapped around a warm cup,
In this festive chaos, we're all lifted up.

So here's to the memories made with glee,
In off-tune caroling, together we're free.
Each note and each laugh, forever will flow,
Through the heartstrings of life, our melodies grow.

The Scent of Pine

The tree is up, it's all a mess,
I swear it twitched, I must confess.
Tinsel fights with all the lights,
As popcorn strands throw silly sights.

Grandma's cookies, oh so grand,
Who knew she'd burn them by a hand?
With every crumb, our laughter grows,
Her secret's out; it's recipe woes.

Uncle Joe wears socks so bold,
One green, one red, a sight to behold.
He claims it's style, we all just grin,
His fashion sense, a holiday win!

So gather 'round and raise a cheer,
For all the quirks that make us dear.
Amidst the wreaths and silly signs,
We cherish each laugh through whiffs of pines.

Flurries of Familiarity

Outside it snows, a fluffy scene,
But inside, chaos reigns supreme.
The dog's in sweaters, oh so proud,
Eating wrapping paper, feeling loud.

The kids build forts, with pillows stacked,
Pinecone missiles all intact.
They launch a volley, giggles flow,
While dad finds peace beneath the snow.

A snowman leans, his head askew,
With sunglasses on and carrot stew.
We argue still, who's best at roles,
While snowflakes dance in winter's strolls.

So let it snow, let laughter fly,
In family ties, we reach the sky.
Through flurries of glee, we find our way,
In quirks and mishaps, we laugh and sway.

Chasing Chilly Breezes

We dash outside, oh what a thrill,
Snowballs fly, it's quite the skill.
A rogue one hits my aunt in the face,
Her shout echoes, we quicken our pace.

The sleds come out, a bumpy ride,
A mix of laughter, and some pride.
But oh, that tree! It blocks our scope,
We sail right by, wish us some hope!

Hot cocoa waits with marshmallows high,
But first, we'll race 'neath the winter sky.
With goofy grins and cheeks all red,
New stories form, while joy's widespread.

As chilly breezes embrace our face,
We scoff at cold with every trace.
Amongst the snow, our hearts do sing,
With each cheeky laugh, the cheer they bring.

Fireside Tales

Gathered 'round with mugs in hand,
We spin old tales, just as we planned.
The cat's on fire, in the stories we weave,
A mythical beast, you won't believe!

Uncle's tales take wild flights,
From ghostly trips to fabulous heights.
We nod along, though half of it's spun,
His stories make us laugh and run.

Grandpa claims he once caught a star,
But it burned out quick, he didn't go far.
With every spill and playful jest,
Our fireside fun is simply the best.

So here we are, with hearts so light,
In cozy vibes that feel just right.
With every laugh that fills the air,
We paint our lives with love and care.

Rustic Roasts and Revelry

In the kitchen, chaos reigns,
Turkey's dancing, gravy's in chains.
Grandma's recipe, a mystery swirl,
We laugh so hard, it gives us a whirl.

A cousin sneezes, and pies take flight,
A fruitcake lands with a surprising bite.
Kids are giggling, they start a food fight,
And somewhere, the cat's taking off into the night.

Lights are twinkling, the tree's askew,
Someone's found eggnog, with a hazy view.
Uncle Joe's stories are all quite the same,
But we roll our eyes; it's part of the game.

Around the table, our hearts beat loud,
Laughter ripples, we're all so proud.
With every bite, we feast and rejoice,
In silly moments, we find our voice.

The Magic of Now

Snowflakes tumble, a beautiful sight,
We throw on our scarves, ready for a fight.
With snowballs flying, laughter fills the air,
We tumble and roll, without a care.

A reindeer costume? Oh dear, what a sight,
Timmy's booked it, full of pure fright.
With every mishap, we chuckle and cheer,
In the chaos of now, all's perfectly clear.

Cards are sent to relatives afar,
But did we write them? Not a single star.
Yet here we gather, no need for display,
Just silly stories and games that we play.

Music's blaring, we dance with no shame,
Even the dog has joined in the game.
In this moment, the joy it will grow,
With laughter and hugs, the true magic flows.

Layers of Love

Gift wrap's tangled; oh what a sight,
Tape is stuck while scissors take flight.
Yet as we wrestle with wrapping galore,
We burst into giggles, then tackle some more.

A secret Santa? Who bought me this sock?
It's part of a joke that truly will rock.
With every layer, surprises unfold,
Memories wrapped in ribbons of gold.

In the pile of chaos, the laughter runs high,
Between silly wishes and heartfelt sighs.
The cookies are burnt, and we start a new batch,
But we don't mind, it's all quite the catch.

So here's to the moments that cause us to grin,
The layers of love where all fun begins.
We may not be perfect, or have it all right,
But together we shine, our spirits so bright.

A Tapestry of Time

A quilt of stories, stitched up with care,
In every corner, there's laughter to share.
Grandpa's old sweater, a curious fit,
When he wore it last, we all have to admit.

With every detail, a chuckle arises,
The mishaps of years, they come as surprises.
Lost presents, tangled lights, such quite a tale,
Yet somehow, through it all, we shall prevail.

Feasting on treats from ages long past,
A fruitcake that's sturdy; it's built to last.
We raise our glasses, cheer loud and clear,
For the tapestry woven with love and with cheer.

With stories remembered, we're forever entwined,
In the fabric of time, we're joyfully aligned.
Through laughter and mishaps, together we climb,
Celebrating each moment, a bright paradigm.

Cherished Glimpses of Yesteryears

In a box of tinsel and cheer,
Old cards and ornaments appear.
Grandpa dressed as Santa, oh my!
With a potato for a pie.

Mom's fruitcake, a timeless delight,
But its texture gave us a fright.
We laughed till we dropped on the floor,
Then ate it all, begging for more.

A cat in a tree, what a scene,
With baubles flying, oh so keen!
After they've scattered, mom would shout,
"Who let the critters all roam about?"

Snowball fights and mittens in pairs,
Hot cocoa spills, and wild stares.
We reminisce, giggling so loud,
As we recall how we were proud.

A Wonderland of Remembered Smiles

A snowman lost half of his head,
An ill-timed thump when he said,
"I'll stand guard and keep out the cold!"
But he melted in sunshine, so bold.

Singing carols, oh what a tune,
Found our voices, a glorious ruin.
Off-key notes, our neighbors would fret,
But who could be mad? We had no regret.

Cookies that looked like reindeer pranced,
With sprinkles that seemed to have danced.
One bite and laughter filled the room,
What was that shape? A mix-up of doom!

The tree's lights flickered, a grand show,
Twinkling brighter, putting on glow.
The dog thought it was a new game,
Chasing shadows, oh what a fame!

Candlelight Reveries

Candle flames flickered with glee,
As we tried to make hot toddy.
But dad spilled it all, oh what a splash,
Now the floor shines with a bright flash.

A sock with a hole, a sight to see,
In the stocking, 'twas meant for me.
Santa must've been in a rush,
To miss the stitching's final hush.

Grandma's wisdom, piecing it right,
"Never wear red with stripes at night."
We giggled and later we sported,
The wildest looks she never imported.

Mirth and laughter filled the air,
As we juggled gifts without care.
Christmas moments, slightly askew,
In our hearts, they'll always feel new.

Echoes of Yesteryear

Remembering the year of the feast,
When a raccoon became our uninvited beast.
He snatched the turkey, oh what a chase,
We laughed till it hurt, embracing the grace.

Silly sweaters worn with great pride,
With reindeer dancing side by side.
A family photo captured the fun,
With mismatched outfits, we're all one!

Hot cider spills and giggles galore,
Mom's secret recipe, we always ignore.
What we think is humor, she just grins,
While we plot for our next holiday wins.

Each memory wrapped in love so bright,
In every mishap, we find the light.
Echoes ringing through laughter and cheer,
Cherishing moments that draw us near.

Tinsel Threads of Time

Once tangled lights brought endless cheer,
A cat in the tree, oh dear!
With popcorn strings and sticky hands,
We danced like reindeer in the bands.

Grandma's cookies, crisp and sweet,
She'd pinch us hard, then say, "You're neat!"
We'd hide the gifts, a sneaky feat,
And search all day, oh what a treat!

Frosty windows, silly faces,
We raced outside in mismatched laces.
Snowball fights with shrieks of glee,
The winner got to sip hot tea!

So here's to cheer and laughter loud,
With every hug, we stand so proud.
These memory threads we tightly weave,
In every heart, they never leave.

Handwritten Letters to the Past

Dear Santa, I hope you're well,
Remember that year? The Christmas spell!
You missed my list, left socks instead,
I still wear them, with pride, it's said.

Mom's fruitcake, oh what a sight,
It bounced right back with all its might!
We laughed until our stomachs hurt,
While plotting how to sneak dessert.

Uncle Joe with his Santa beard,
His ho-ho-ho seemed slightly weird.
He tripped on lights, went for a fall,
We couldn't help but burst at all!

So here's my note, a giggle or two,
Thank you for joy, and mischief too!
I'll cherish the moments, the silly fun,
In every letter, our hearts are one.

Snowflakes on Forgotten Laughs

Falling flakes, like laughter's end,
We made snowmen round the bend.
A carrot nose? Oh what a plan!
Till it melted on Uncle Stan.

Hot cocoa spills, a race to sip,
Marshmallow battles at every trip.
With sticky hands and powdered nose,
We'd dream of snow forts where joy grows.

Each winter evening, stories spun,
Of reindeer games and Christmas fun.
We'd giggle loud, then fade to dreams,
While winter whispered, or so it seems.

So let us dance in snowflakes light,
Recalling moments that feel so right.
Through all the cheer and playful scoff,
These forgotten laughs, we'll never scoff.

Nostalgic Nights Under Starlit Skies

Under the tree, we hid with glee,
Whispers of wishes, just you and me.
A knock on the door, who's it to be?
Santa or a neighbor's pet, oh what a spree!

With paper hats and silly tunes,
We danced along to the silly boons.
The clock struck twelve, oh what a fright,
We stayed up long past midnight's light.

Remember the time you tripped and fell?
We couldn't help but laugh so well.
With blankets piled and a game in hand,
The joy we share, oh isn't it grand?

So gather 'round, let stories unwind,
In every chuckle, a treasure we find.
Here's to the nights we'll never forget,
With stars above, our hearts are set.

Starlit Reflections

Twinkling lights on the tree, oh how they glow,
Mismatched socks, oh where did they go?
Cookies stuck to the roof of my mouth,
Santa's on the roof, and he's heading south!

Grandma's fruitcake, a hefty old brick,
Uncles arguing if it's a gift or a trick.
Snowball fights with dad, he slips on the path,
Laughing so hard, I forgot what I hath!

Recalled all the mishaps we had through the years,
Like Auntie's hat flying and dad's frozen tears.
Every little moment now makes us grin,
With gifts and a whole lot of laughter to spin!

So here's to the holidays, silly and bright,
With memories cherished, that stretch through the night.
Let's toast with warm cocoa, so sweet and so dear,
To the joy of the season, and friends bringing cheer!

Voices of the Past

Echoes of laughter from my childhood days,
Overcooked turkey, and Aunt Bea's wild ways.
Pine needles stuck in my hair, oh what a sight,
Giggles and snorts late into the night!

Tales from old folks, some truth, some a fib,
Like cousin Ed's dog that once swallowed a rib.
The lights flicker out as we sing off-key,
Yet every off-note is pure harmony!

Snowmen crafted with faces that melt,
Grumbling about sweaters, oh how they felt!
The smell of hot chocolate wafts through the air,
As we reminisce how we once had no care.

Loud cheers for the games that never went right,
Knocking down ornaments, oh what a fright.
So let's toast to the past, with a wink and a cheer,
For the voices that echo so vividly here!

Sledding into Memory Lane

Sledding down hills with a whoop and a shout,
Spinning and tumbling, we laughed all about.
The snowball fight led to one epic war,
While mom sipped her tea, her eyes rolling for sure!

Face-first in snow, an issue so grand,
Cousins all laughing, unable to stand.
The sledge built for two, but it's way too small,
Hilarious crash, we just can't help but fall!

Frostbite on fingers, hot cocoa so near,
Sharing wild stories, we couldn't help but cheer.
As elves in the kitchen bake pies with a flair,
The metrics of chaos—oh, they truly compare!

So here's to the joy that the season bestows,
Like snowflakes falling—each one uniquely glows.
These moments we treasure, oh can't you just see?
That sledding brings back such fond history!

Shadows of the Season

In the gloom of the night, with shadows so bended,
Broke a bauble, oh how it was ended!
Dad's dance with the broom, a sight that we loved,
As laughter erupted from the skies above!

Twinkling lights swaying, a clumsy old game,
Mom tripped on trimmings, we all felt the shame.
Uncle Joe's jokes, a whirlwind of cheer,
Though half of them came with a side of a sneer!

Whispers of yams, the burnt crispy kind,
Recipes lost in the chaos of mind.
Misplacing the gifts, so predictable—why?
But hope springs eternal when the eggnog runs dry!

So as we gather, hold dear every laugh,
Each fumble and blunder makes a beautiful path.
For in shadows of laughter, we find what we miss,
Those memories brightened with a holiday bliss!

Heartstrings and Holly

Beneath the mistletoe we stood,
Uncle Joe forgot the good food.
He tried to bake a ginger bread,
But ended up with something dead.

Laughter echoes in the halls,
Silly hats and jingle bells call.
Crazy sweaters all too bright,
Fighting over who has the best sight.

The cat finds comfort in the tree,
A festive spot, or so it believes.
With baubles hanging like fragile dreams,
It's now a toy, or so it seems.

Cookies left out in a hurry,
Santa comes, no time to worry.
He takes a bite, then shakes his head,
And leaves a note - "I'm gluten-free instead!"

When Time Stood Still

Remember when we dressed up the pup?
Ribbons and bows, oh what a setup!
He ran away, a hilarious sight,
Chasing squirrels in pure delight.

The tree stood tall, a dazzling glow,
But with one crash, all joy hit low.
Ornaments flew as the dog dashed by,
And we laughed so hard we nearly cried.

Grandma's eggnog was a strong blend,
And she kept pouring, it was hard to pretend.
She danced like a queen, so full of cheer,
We hoped her two left feet would disappear.

Snow turned to mud when the kids all came,
"Snowball fights!" they shouted, oh what a game.
In the end we soaked, all drenched with joy,
And laughed at the chaos that plagues every boy.

Soft Whispers of Winter

Whispers of snowflakes fall so slow,
Yet the kids run wild, what a show!
Building snowmen with lopsided heads,
But they aren't fierce, just silly spreads.

Our pajamas are bright, with reindeer and more,
Somehow they're stuck at the local store.
"Who wore it best?" becomes the debate,
As we pose, giggling, it feels like fate.

Sledding adventures down the street,
Until someone lands on their feet.
Mom's hot chocolate is a gooey delight,
She adds some marshmallows, yes, that's just right.

The fire crackles, we roast our treats,
Forget about worries, life's little feats.
Cousins argue over who's the best chef,
While we munch on leftovers, proof of our heft.

The Glow of Yule

Candles glowing with flickering light,
Mom's apple pie, oh, such a sight!
We make a toast with fizzy juice,
Toasting a year that's been mostly goose.

The pets wear antlers, they look so proud,
Trying to blend in with the family crowd.
They steal the show, and well, the treats,
Catching crumbs from our festive feats.

Dancing around with a mix of glee,
Twirling and whirling, let's spill some tea!
Granddad's old stories, we roll our eyes,
But in our hearts, we cherish the lies.

In this chaos, magic does unfold,
Winter tales worth more than gold.
With laughter ringing, the memories blend,
We promise again, this joy will not end.

Cocoa-Kissed Remembrances

A mug of cocoa, piled high with cream,
Marshmallows floating, it's a sweet dream.
Grandpa tells tales, with a wink and a grin,
While the cat's in the tree, counting all his sins.

Snowmen stacked high, but one lost his nose,
The dog ate it up, now he's in the prose.
We laugh and we giggle, with hearts full of cheer,
As auntie busts out her infamous reindeer.

The lights twinkle bright, like stars pure and true,
But the tinsel's a battle, conquered by the cat too.
With laughter and joy, we feast on those pies,
The echoes of giggles are the best Christmas prize.

So here's to the moments of joy and delight,
With cocoa and friends, everything feels right.
We'll cherish these days, the funny and sweet,
In the heart of the season, oh what a treat.

Evergreen Heartstrings

The tree's decorated with odd little things,
Toilet paper garlands, how laughter it brings.
With twinkling lights blinking like disco at night,
Aunt Sue in the corner is too merry to fight.

Uncle Joe's dancing, the cat leaps away,
He thinks he's a pro in this festive ballet.
Each ornament tells a peculiar old tale,
Of last year's mishaps that never grow stale.

We gather 'round feasts of cookies and cheer,
But find every plate is just crumbs, oh dear!
With faces gaudy from icing so sweet,
We giggle through bites, oh, this love is a treat.

So raise a glass high to our quirks and our charm,
To moments when mischief keeps us safe from harm.
With evergreen heartstrings and laughter in play,
We weave a fine tapestry, year after year stays.

Lanterns Flicker with Echoes

Lanterns aglow, flickering bright,
In the attic of memories, they twinkle tonight.
Grandma sings carols, a tune that's a hoot,
It sounds like a rooster in search of its route.

On the porch, we hang socks, all mismatched, it seems,
Wishing for gifts like we're living in dreams.
But all that we find is a lump on the floor,
Looks like bumbling Santa forgot once more!

The cookies go missing, each year it's the same,
The dog's wearing reindeer horns—oh, what a game!
With laughter and love sprouting strong from our hearts,
These moments unwrapped are the best kind of arts.

So let's keep the lanterns all brightly aglow,
While we dance 'round the room, with a dash of true show.
The echoes of joy will ring through the night,
And with daily mischief, our spirits take flight.

Mistletoe Dreams Beneath the Hearth

Mistletoe dangling, a critter's delight,
Uncle Tom puckers, it's quite a silly sight.
With giggles and grins, we all gather near,
Expecting some magic, yet laughter is clear.

There's a pot on the fire, a stew far too bold,
A sprinkle of chaos, or so I've been told.
We dive into food with a clatter and clang,
While Aunt Mary insists, "Just taste the dang sang!"

Outside, the snowflakes join in on the mess,
Fluffy white piles mean a day full of stress.
We roll in the cold, with our cheeks nice and red,
While stories of chaos dance 'round in our head.

So here's to the laughter, the fun and the play,
To hearth-side adventures that brighten our day.
With mistletoe wishes and memories that bloom,
We'll count every giggle as we light up the room.

The Heart of the Hearth

In the kitchen, cookies burn,
Mom's wine spills, 'Oh, wait your turn!'
Reindeer antlers on the dog,
As he snorts and hogs the log.

Grandma's sweater, bright and loud,
Almost outshining the crowd.
A cat in a Santa hat,
Plotting mischief, imagine that!

Uncle Joe with mistletoe,
Stumbles, falls – oh no, oh no!
Laughter echoes through the night,
'Twas a jolly, silly sight!

In our hearts, the cheer will stay,
Even if socks lead the way.
Nights like these spark joy again,
With big smiles, we'll do it ten!

Woven Wishes

Tinsel tangled in my hair,
'Tis the season, but beware!
Cookies stacked in piles so high,
I'm just hoping not to die!

The tree leans, what a show,
Its lights flicker, put on a glow.
Pine needles on the floor abound,
It's like a forest all around!

Auntie's hat's a sight to see,
She says it's warmth, I just say, 'Flee!'
Amidst the laughter and the cheer,
I'll find the pie, now that's sincere!

A toast to family, oh so bright,
With every blooper, pure delight.
Through the fun, we find our way,
Blessed are those who choose to stay!

Pastel Hues of the Holidays

Snowflakes fall in shades of pink,
While kids complain, 'I can't even think!'
Gingerbread houses, oh what fun,
Until you bite and break your bun!

Candy canes stuck in my hair,
I won't deny I had a scare.
Friends all gather round to cheer,
As mashed potatoes disappear!

Mom's new thing? Bright neon lights,
That turn our house into blinding sights.
And every blooper fills the room,
With warm hearts in the holiday bloom!

In laughter's glow, we sing off-key,
Dancing like there's no degree.
Amidst bright hues and joyful shifts,
It's laughter here that truly lifts!

Serenity Beneath the Snow

Beneath the flakes, a truce we find,
Snowball fights, oh how unkind!
The sledding hill, my epic fall,
As everyone laughs, I stand tall.

With cocoa spills and marshmallow clouds,
We gather 'round, a chirpy crowd.
Corny jokes fly through the air,
Granny's puns, no one can bear!

A puppy wrestles with a scarf,
Dodging mittens, he's truly daft.
Tinsel and giggles mix as one,
Creating memories full of fun!

So in this season, let's embrace,
Every awkward, funny face.
Through all the quirks one thing stays,
Joy remains in silly ways!

Fireside Whispers

By the fire, the socks are lacking,
Grandpa's snoring, we're all cracking.
The cat's seen fit to steal a treat,
While Auntie spills her drink on her feet.

The chestnuts roast with quite a flair,
Uncle Joe's dance is beyond compare.
The kids are giggling, pets in tow,
As marshmallows bounce in the ember's glow.

Cousin Lucy's wearing curtains as a dress,
Her fashion choice is a hot mess,
But laughter fills this bustling space,
And joy is worn upon each face.

In these moments, silly and bright,
We hold our memories, tight and right.
With whispers shared from near and far,
These fireside tales shine like a star.

Echoes of Yuletide Joy

In the kitchen, there's such a show,
As Grandma's cookies start to flow.
With flour clouds and frosting fights,
We laugh 'til we cry on chilly nights.

The tree is lopsided, ornaments askew,
Uncle's convinced it's a grand debut.
While lights flicker with a curious spark,
The dog thinks it's a late night lark.

Snowballs fly; the carolers croon,
While Grandma hums an off-tune tune.
The echoes linger, sweet and strange,
These memories, oh! How they rearrange.

So here's a toast, with cocoa cups,
To all the fun and silly hiccups.
In every giggle and every cheer,
The spirit of the season is here!

Glistening Moments in December's Glow

Twinkling lights wrapped on the cat,
Dad trips over, oh, imagine that!
The tinsel's tangled in a great big mess,
But laughter follows, no need to stress.

Cookies crumble, chocolate galore,
While kids sneak bites and then ignore.
The smell of pine fills up the room,
As snowflakes fall, we all can bloom.

Grandpa's jokes are outdated, it's true,
But we laugh hard, that's what we do.
The fun we have is worth more than gold,
As stories are shared and memories unfold.

These moments shine bright like festive lights,
Creating warmth on the coldest nights.
We cherish the humor, love, and cheer,
In December's glow, we hold it dear.

Cinnamon and Cradle Songs

Cinnamon swirls through the kitchen air,
While Dad and the kids start a playful dare.
The pie is baking, but so is the fun,
With laughter and joy until we're done.

Auntie croons a lullaby or two,
The baby giggles, what's she gonna do?
While grandpa spins tales of Christmas past,
All the while, the snowy wind blasts.

Hot chocolate spills on Grandma's chair,
But she just laughs with love to spare.
The cloud of marshmallows floats so high,
As we clink our mugs, "Here's to the sky!"

From silly to sweet, our hearts align,
In these moments, we richly dine.
For within these walls of merriment and song,
We find where all of us belong.

Milton Keynes UK
Ingram Content Group UK Ltd.
UKHW020818141124
451205UK00012B/635

Original title:
The Warmth of Christmas Memories

Copyright © 2024 Creative Arts Management OÜ
All rights reserved.

Author: Kieran Blackwood
ISBN HARDBACK: 978-9916-94-062-4
ISBN PAPERBACK: 978-9916-94-063-1

Scribbled Wishes in the Snow

Snowflakes dancing on my nose,
I build a snowman, with big blue toes.
He wobbles and flops with a grin so wide,
Yet down he goes for a slippery slide.

Hot cocoa spills on my winter socks,
I slip on ice while walking, oh what a shock!
Laughter echoes as I tumble right,
Guess I'll stick to the warmth inside tonight!

Voices of Winter's Embrace

Carolers sing off-key by the tree,
Their voices crack like a festive decree.
Santa's sleigh got stuck in the snow,
He's shouting, 'More reindeer, let's make it go!'

Grandma's cookies are lopsided and burnt,
Yet every bite, my taste buds are spurned.
We munch and we laugh, oh what a scene,
Celebrating flavors that defy the routine!

Cradles of Childhood Cheer

Racing down the hallway, my socks a blur,
I trip and I tumble, but what's the deter?
Presents are hiding, oh where can they be?
I'll dive in the pile, just wait and see!

A game with the cat, he swats at the bow,
It's a questionable gift, but what does he know?
Amidst all the chaos and playful delight,
These shenanigans sparkle, so merry and bright!

A Tapestry of Twinkling Lights

Twinkling bulbs flash in a dazzle so loud,
I trip on the cord, what a clumsy proud!
The tree stands tall, but lopsided for sure,
O Christmas, you silly, who knew you'd allure?

Rudolph's nose blinks like a disco ball,
While Uncle Bob dances, we all start to fall.
Jingle bells ringing, and laughter ignites,
This festive fiasco is pure holiday sights!

Time-Honored Traditions

Grandma's fruitcake, dense as a brick,
We all took a bite, it made us all sick.
Uncle Joe snores loud, like a grizzly bear,
Only to wake up, with frosting in hair.

Tree covered in tinsel, a glittery mess,
We'd blame the cat when it's time to confess.
Ornaments tangled, like lights in a knot,
Dad says, "It's fine, just takes a good shot!"

Notes of Nostalgia

Singing off-key to carols so bright,
Then tripping on boots, that gave us a fright.
Pine-scented air mixed with mom's hot stew,
Made us all giggle like the joy was brand new.

Wrapping up gifts that were slightly too late,
Last year's presents? Well, they still look great!
We'd joke and we'd laugh, with our hearts full of cheer,
Unwrapping each one, like it's just disappeared.

Yesterday's Laughter

Santa got stuck in the flue, what a sight,
We pulled him out, but he gave us a fright.
With cookies all crumbled, and milk spilled about,
We laughed till our bellies were round as a bout.

Snowball fights turned into snow-tastrophes,
Sledding downhill was a total mischief.
One tumble and roll, we'd all hit the slush,
Laughter erupted, in the frosty rush.

Cloaked in Comfort

Grandpa's old sweater, three sizes too large,
He wore it with pride like he's leading a charge.
Hot cocoa spills and marshmallows afloat,
A funny mix-up like the Christmas we wrote.

Midnight snacks claimed by a sneaky raccoon,
We found him munching beneath the full moon.
Laughter erupted, as he made his escape,
With a cocoa mustache, and a sweet little shape.

Memories Wrapped in Ribbons

A box of lights with tangled strings,
A cat naps soundly, dreaming of things.
Mom's slippers go flying, it's quite the show,
As Uncle Joe dances, despite the snow.

Grandma's old eggnog sits on the shelf,
With a hint of spice, it confuses itself.
Cousins all giggle at the fruitcake surprise,
While a snowman outside wears dad's old ties.

Socks that don't match, oh what a sight,
We toast with hot cocoa, the mood feels just right.
Tickles and laughter, all around the room,
As we cherish these times, let the silly bloom.

Toasts to Togetherness

We raise our mugs in a joyful cheer,
Grandpa starts teasing, we always want to hear.
A toast for each cousin, and one for the dog,
Who's hiding their treats under the old fog.

The roast's gone rogue, on the floor it's found,
Oh, what a family! Just sit back, astound.
Silly stories are shared as we dig right in,
With Auntie's last mishap and Uncle's old grin.

Laughter erupts at the silliest tales,
Of snowball fights ending with snow-covered veils.
Cookies baked badly, but smiles remain,
Hands raised together, through joy and through pain.

Snowflake Stories

Outside it is snowing, a magical scene,
While inside we're busy with cookies and cream.
Sledding adventures, a face full of snow,
Caught on the camera, so funny to show.

Cousins are twirling, a conga-line spree,
And someone gets tangled, oh what a sight to see!
Frosty's a legend, but he drifts with the wind,
And dad learned to snowboard, now that's how it's pinned.

Among all the giggles, a story is told,
Of snowball wars fought brave, valiant, and bold.
With gifts by the fireside, both big and small,
We have our tales mixed with laughter and all.

Warm Winks of Winter

The fireplace crackles, with magical sparks,
As Grandma swoops in, yelling, "Who's stole the tarts?"
A wink and a smile from each little face,
Holding a secret, in this warm winter space.

The kids are all dressed like giant marshmallows,
Sleds flying fast while the laughter just bellows.
Mom trips on the carpet, and down goes her drink,
We all burst with giggles, hey, what do you think?

Pine needles scatter, as we deck out the tree,
In ornaments silly, matching none of we.
With cocoa in hand, that's where joy combines,
And every sweet moment like glitter just shines.

A Melody of Memories

Jingle bells clatter, a cat takes a seat,
Stuck on the tree, oh what a feat!
Granddad's still singing his off-key tune,
While grandma's lost track of the nice and the rude.

Mittens piled high, a snowball fight,
Uncle Joe's aim was not quite right.
The snowman looks worried, his hat's a bit crooked,
As we sip hot cocoa and munch on the cookied.

Coziness and Cheer

Socks on the fire, what a great place,
They're popping and cracking, we make a race.
The lights are all blinking, the dog's in a loop,
Chasing his tail, oh what a goof troop!

Ribbons of laughter, so bright in the air,
Dad trips on the garland, oh no, it's a scare!
A pie in the oven, who should we blame?
Mom said she'd bake it, it's not the same!

Emblazed in Laughter

Each gift a surprise, the wrapping is bright,
A present for me? Oh, what a delight!
But wait, it's just socks with a glittery view,
The gift that keeps giving, from Aunt Sue, it's true!

Cookies for Santa, or so I thought,
But Rudolph just ate them, now I'm left fraught.
No milk in the fridge, a glass of old tea,
This Christmas may just end in a comedy spree!

Solstice Serenades

Carols are ringing, off-key but loud,
The neighbors all laugh, they're quite the crowd.
Harold's dance moves, a little bizarre,
He'll surely be famous, in a weird way, so far!

Eggnog spills over, our favorite drink,
It could double as glue, oh what do you think?
Laughter erupts, the magic is clear,
This silly old gathering is one we hold dear.

A Warmth That Lingers

In socks mismatched, we dance with glee,
The lights that twinkle, a sight to see.
Grandma's fruitcake, oh what a treat,
Even the cat says, "This can't be beat!"

We sip hot cocoa, marshmallow fluff,
Mom's telling stories, though we've heard enough.
The dog steals a roll, to our surprise,
As we all burst out laughing, tears in our eyes.

Gathering Around the Glowing Hearth

Gathered close, with blankets thick,
Uncle Joe starts his magic trick.
With a hat and a rabbit, he's lost his mind,
The rabbit hops off — no one can find!

The fire crackles, sparks fly high,
We roast marshmallows, oh me, oh my!
S'mores are devoured, sticky and sweet,
As Dad yells, "Fire!" — it's just our feet!

Chasing Shadows of Festive Echoes

Snowmen stand tall, with smiles so wide,
But one got a pumpkin, what a bizarre ride!
Carrot noses, eyes of coal,
In the yard, a Santa with a roll!

We chase shadows, giggling, carefree,
The neighbors peek out, oh, who could it be?
It's just us kids, a mischief-filled crew,
With reindeer antics, and a sled that flew!

Gifts of Time Tied with Ribbons

With ribbon untied, the chaos begins,
We're all on a hunt — who wins?
A box labeled "Yarn" contains a rat,
A gift from Aunt Sue — no one saw that!

We unwrap the laughter, layer by layer,
Each present a puzzle, let's be a player.
As paper flies, it's a joyful mess,
A Christmas so weird, who could guess less?

Unraveled Gifts

The ribbons flew like birds in flight,
Hiding snacks, oh what a sight!
Wrapped so tight, the paper screamed,
Hope you like what I dreamed!

A box of socks, a rubber duck,
Thought I'd fill it with my luck!
I gave you sweets, you gave me chills,
With every bite, we got our thrills!

Portraits of Peace

In sweaters bright, we pose and grin,
 Next year, let's aim for the win!
Dad's beard caught in the cookie jar,
 Merry chaos, it's our bizarre!

A picture taken, faces misaligned,
 Mom's hairdo—what a find!
Capture the night with spicy cheer,
Snapshot of laughter through the year!

Savoring Sweet Moments

Cookies stacked like towers high,
Oops! One fell, oh my, oh my!
Milk spilled like magic tricks,
Giggling kids with sticky licks!

A feast begins, but wait, what's this?
The cat stole pie, it's such pure bliss!
We laugh and munch on all that's here,
Sweet moments like this, oh dear!

Childhood Echoes

The snowballs fly, oh how they flew,
Remember when we hit Aunt Sue?
Laughter ringing in the snowy air,
As frosty flakes tangled in our hair!

With sleds that tipped and cheeks so red,
We'd race till we crashed and fell, instead!
Those echoes of giggles, a fantasy,
Hold them close, they're pure jubilee!

Snowy Embraces

Snowflakes dance like crazy crowds,
While we chase them like little kids,
With snowmen dressed in mismatched clothes,
And carrots that forget where they hid.

Hot cocoa spills on my brand new coat,
As marshmallows float like fluffy dreams,
Uncle Joe slipped on the icy path,
And fell right into mom's yarn schemes.

We sing off-key, it's a joyous sound,
Mistletoe hangs above our heads,
Nan's cookies are as hard as bricks,
Yet we eat them all, just like she said.

Amid the laughter and goofy brawls,
We cherish moments, though some are loud,
Each snowy hug and silly fall,
Leaves a smile that's winter proud.

Treasures of the Heart

A gift that's wrapped with sparkly tape,
Looks fancy but holds a plastic toy,
Granddad chuckles at our surprise,
"Best secret ever!" says our boy.

The cat leaps up, oh what a mess,
With ribbons wrapped 'round her tiny paws,
She thinks it's all a game to play,
While we shout and give her applause.

A fruitcake sits, a family curse,
With layers that could stop a car,
Yet every year, we slice a piece,
Making legends of our bizarre.

The stories shared around the tree,
Are treasures that fill our hearts with cheer,
With laughter echoing through the night,
We gather close, year after year.

Yule Legends Revisited

The elf on the shelf, he's up to tricks,
He dances on the TV with glee,
While we're convinced that he's watching us,
Is he a spy or just goofy?

Stockings stuffed with socks and sweets,
Mom's got an eye for crafty seams,
Dad forgets to take a hint,
When asked to fix those broken dreams.

We gather 'round with lights aglow,
As Grandpa nods off in his chair,
Then wakes with tales from long ago,
Of Christmas magic that fills the air.

Each legend fills our hearts with joy,
As we swap tales and share more laughs,
With each new tale, our spirits soar,
Brother takes charge of the silly crafts.

Frost-Kissed Hues

The tree is crooked—it leans to one side,
With tinsel that looks like a bird's nest,
Ornaments swinging in a wild ride,
While the angel on top gets no rest.

Chilly winds whistle through the streets,
As we try to build a snow fort high,
But all we create is a slushy mess,
Guess the snowball fight is worth a try.

Grandma's sweater is two sizes too big,
In colors that clash like a wild dream,
She loves it still—the warmth it brings,
While we try not to giggle and scream.

With mischief brewing, the night takes flight,
As we recount tales with twinkling eyes,
In these frosty hues filled with laughter,
Are the lovely moments, our greatest prize.

Mistletoe Moments

Under the mistletoe, I made my move,
Tripped on my feet, what a funny groove!
Kissed a dear aunt who wore red lipstick,
Now I sport a print that's quite the trick.

Grandpa told jokes, oh, how they did soar,
Laughed until we fell, rolling on the floor!
A cat stole the scene, with a Christmas bow,
Lurking by the snack—oh, what a show!

A Gathering of Hearts

Family around, with stories to share,
Uncle Sam's tales, a wild, wacky flair!
Sister's new dance looks like a spastic move,
We laugh till we cry, can't help but approve.

Cousins all gathered, a photo we take,
But one of us blinked—watch that funny face break!
Gifts wrapped in layers, with endless tape,
Now we're stuck in a paper-slicing escape!

Gingerbread Dreams

Baked a gingerbread house, it leaned to the side,
The roof caved in, surprised we all cried!
I took a big bite, frosting on my nose,
Santa's not the only one with the joy that he shows.

Cookies went missing, who could it be?
The dog gave a glance, as guilty as can be!
Sprinkles on his snout, icing in his fur,
Is this canine a chef? Oh, what a stir!

Cocoa and Comfort

Cocoa in hand, I warmed up my soul,
But spilled it on Grandma, oh, how I roll!
She laughed so hard, the mug in her grip,
Now she's the one with hot chocolate on her lip.

Marshmallows floating, kids on the floor,
Bouncing around like never before!
A blanket fort made, it's cozy and bright,
But where's the cocoa? Oh, what a sight!

Sledding Down Memory Lane

Snowy hills were our playground,
We raced with laughter, face full of cold.
Sleds that flew like parachutes,
Landing in piles, stories untold.

Hot cocoa spills on mom's new chair,
Marshmallow fights, giggles and cheer.
We dressed like penguins, layers galore,
With hats so big, we could barely steer.

Mittens soaked from snowball wars,
Friction burns from sledding too fast.
But who needs warmth when you've got friends,
To laugh through chilly moments amassed.

Days like these, tangled in glee,
Noses pink under twinkling lights.
Who knew sledding could feel so grand,
With memories stored in snowy heights.

Fond Embraces Wrapped in Brightness

Auntie's hugs, like marshmallows puffed,
Squeeze too tight, you can't escape.
Her perfume smells like peppermint dreams,
Wrapped up tightly, escaping the drape.

Christmas lights blink in rhythm divine,
We twirled under stars from the attic.
Grandma's cookies, burnt just a tad,
But love made all the flavors ecstatic.

Uncle Joe's dance, such a sight!
Two left feet, but he owns the floor.
His reindeer antlers fall to the ground,
Making our sides split, hearts wanting more.

In the chaos, we find our peace,
Mom's laughter floats, joyous and bright.
Wrapped in hugs, and banter so sweet,
Family felt like magic that night.

Holly and Hope in Gentle Hues

Bright ribbons wrapped around laughter,
Holly hung asking for a kiss.
Grandpa reads with a twinkle, how sweet,
Stories that promise a little bliss.

Wrapping paper, a shimmery mess,
Cats dive in with no ounce of shame.
Presents tossed like snowflakes adrift,
Who needs toys when the cat's the game?

Ballet slippers dance with delight,
A tree decorated with eco-style.
Out of the box, our dreams take flight,
We leap and spin, all dressed with a smile.

Memories twinkle like ornaments hung,
In every crackle, a chuckle hides.
While holly and color bring us together,
It's the quirks that make our joy wide.

Echoing Laughter Through Frosted Windows

Frosted panes show our antics bold,
Snowmen with noses, shriveled and small.
We posed for pictures, stuck out our tongues,
Hoping the snow wouldn't end in a brawl.

Outside the world froze in silent bliss,
While inside we ate all the treats.
Nibbled on cookies, frosting on noses,
Racing each other for seconds and feats.

Muffin disasters, flour in the air,
Mom's face a mix of love and dismay.
Fire crackles, bringing warmth so tight,
Who needs a recipe? We play! We play!

Laughter echoes through frosted frames,
Each giggle a gift, fresh and bright.
Time stands still, in this cheerful realm,
Where memories glow like the stars at night.

Family Ties and Twinkling Lights

Gather round the fabled tree,
Where chaos swirls, oh can't you see?
Uncle Joe brings "holiday cheer,"
With laughter spilling in his beer.

Aunt May's fruitcake, hard as stone,
Leaves everyone to groan and moan.
But in the corner, kids conspire,
To set the cat's tail on fire!

The lights are dim, the bulbs are bright,
Grandpa's snoring, what a sight!
While stories told take odd twists,
And we all ponder, 'Did we exist?'

Gathered close with warmth inside,
Swapped old tales we cannot hide.
As magic swirls in silly flights,
These moments glow like twinkling lights.

Keeping Christmas Close

Sneaky Santa, what a tale,
Wrapped in jokes that never fail.
Our secret stash of tasty treats,
I see you nibbling on the sweets!

With mismatched socks, we all parade,
Into the living room, unafraid.
Grandma's punch, all spicy and nice,
A potent brew; we pay the price!

The tree is wobbling side to side,
Each ornament's a sloshed ride.
As laughter dances through the air,
I swear I saw a flying chair!

With goofy hats and silly songs,
We've turned it up; we can't go wrong.
In every hug, a quirky boast,
This time of year, we love the most.

Remnants of Yuletide Joy

Beneath the lights, we gather round,
As old tunes play, a timeless sound,
And Grandma's knitted hats, mismatched,
Are what our joyous hearts have hatched.

The cookies burned, a crispy fate,
Yet still we laugh and contemplate.
Uncle Fred tried to gift us all,
A singing fish, it made us fall!

With grand tales told of Christmas past,
We share the giggles, make them last,
As secrets spill from mouths agape,
Like Grandpa's antics, what a shape!

Through all the love, and laughter's grace,
These silly moments, we embrace.
In every glimmer, laughter's near,
Our hearts ring loud with festive cheer!

Ancestral Cheer

With cousin cards that all are wrong,
We sit back, laughing all night long.
A feast so grand, who could survive?
There's turkey leg and pie, oh my!

A game of charades turns to mayhem,
As Auntie shrieks, "You'll never tame him!"
Dressed up as elves, we laugh and play,
Our family shenanigans on display.

Uncle's jokes, they never end,
As every punchline twists a bend.
With eggnog spills and jolly roars,
We keep returning for more and more.

In cozy hugs, our hearts expand,
Through silly stories, hand in hand.
With love and laughter, it is clear,
This is the season we all hold dear.

Milestones in Mirth

A cat in a hat, what a sight,
Chasing paper balls, oh what delight!
Grandma slipped on the ice with grace,
Now she's the star of our family space.

Uncle Bob's dance, quite the show,
Spilled his drink all over Joe.
We laughed until our sides would ache,
A Christmas to remember, make no mistake!

The turkey's burnt, but we don't care,
We gobble up cookies, in our chairs,
A battle of snowballs, who'll take the prize?
Laughter erupts as the snow monster lies.

With tinsel hair and a jingle bell,
We've spun around like a carousel.
In moments like these, love fills the air,
Memories knitted, beyond compare.

Silhouettes of Celebration

Tinsel stuck on the dog's tail,
He runs like the wind, a furry snail.
A mishap with lighting, oh what a scene,
We lit up the house like a bad Halloween!

Grandpa's snoring under the tree,
With a cookie stash, as happy as can be.
Sister sings off-key, what a cheer,
We hand her a mic, she's the star here!

Reindeer games that went awry,
A flying sleigh ride, nearly to the sky.
We laughed 'til we cried, can't keep track,
Of who wore the antlers, and who wore the sack.

In the warmth of the room, jokes fly around,
Echoes of laughter, the best kind of sound.
We celebrate quirks that make us whole,
In each silly moment, love's the goal.

Threads of Togetherness

Knitting sweaters far too tight,
We all look like sausages tonight!
A cheer when the cookies somehow flop,
"Let's order pizza!" — Oh, what a swap!

Grandma's putting marshmallows in stew,
We debate if that's something we'd do.
A game of charades, hilariously poor,
We act like penguins, and then roll on the floor!

In a mix of laughter, joy floods the night,
With inside jokes that feel just right.
A gift from last year, still in the wrap,
"Is this my old sweater?" it's all a trap!

With friends and family, we gather close,
Counting the blessings that matter most.
In funny mishaps, we find our cheer,
In the love we share, we hold most dear.

Whispers in the Wind

A snowman fell and rolled away,
Chasing after him was quite the play.
Our snowflakes' battle, a frosty war,
And hot cocoa spills on the kitchen floor!

There's a sock on the cat — what a funny sight,
As he struts through the room, all filled with delight.
Dad's got candy canes stuck in his beard,
"It's all part of Christmas," he proudly cheered!

Slippers on the dog, he's a merry sight,
Barking at bells that jingle all night.
We tell silly stories, and laugh 'til we cry,
As the moon shines bright in the frosty sky.

Around the table, our hearts are aglow,
With tales of mishaps in the recent snow.
Each chuckle, each grin, a gift that we lend,
In the spirit of joy, our hearts never end.

Echoes Beneath the Stars

Twinkling lights and silly hats,
We danced with dogs and sang with cats.
Grandma's fruitcake, a brick in disguise,
We laughed so hard, tears filled our eyes.

The sleigh ride went off a tiny cliff,
Santa yelled, 'Hey, where's my gift?'
Mistletoe hung way too high,
We all got stuck, oh my, oh my!

Frosty melted, oh what a shame,
He slipped on ice while playing a game.
We built him back with half a grin,
He winked at us, let the fun begin!

In memory's vault, joy holds the key,
Each goofy mishap, a gem, you see.
Under the stars, we raise a cheer,
For laughter shared, the best time of year!

The Hearthstone Haven

Gathered 'round the fire's glow,
Uncle Joe lost track of his toe.
He wore a sock that looked like this:
A reindeer's face, we couldn't miss!

Cookies vanished in a blink,
Elves must've come, we start to think.
Dad filled his eggnog, oh so bold,
Now he's dancing like he's five years old.

Watching the cat chase tinsel strings,
He thought he'd caught all the shiny things.
With each pounce and jump, our hearts would race,
Turns out he just wanted a cozy place.

The warmth of laughter fills the room,
As stories swirl like a fragrant plume.
Around the hearth, we share a grin,
Thanking fortune for the joyful din.

Flickering Firelight

In firelight's glow, the stories blend,
Of turkey mishaps and a sock that bend.
Mom's soufflé soared up to its height,
Then dropped like it lost its will to fight.

Cousin Larry in a Santa suit,
He couldn't fit through the front, oh, shoot!
We had a laugh, he wriggled away,
With sparkly lights, signs of dismay.

Hiding gifts became a grand old time,
I found a sweater that looked like a crime.
Neighbors peeked in with a curious glare,
'What's with that outfit? Just don't compare!'

Through flickering flames, memories rise,
With silly tales and starry skies.
We gather tight, our hearts in tune,
Creating magic beneath the moon.

Branches of the Past

Decking the halls with mismatched flair,
Some ornaments hung with delicate care.
Yet a cat played hide-and-seek in the tree,
Somersaults down — oh, what a spree!

The gifts were wrapped with duct tape woes,
Dad couldn't find where the ribbon goes.
A gingerbread house made of pure delight,
But someone nibbled it, oh, what a sight!

Forgotten socks in the Santa sack,
A mystery box we just can't keep track.
Labels askew, names in a spin,
We've learned by now, chaos must win.

Branching through laughter, we reminisce,
Each goofy moment, a hug we don't miss.
In every cheer that echoes near,
We hold those quirks so dear, so dear.

Stories Spun by the Fire's Glare

The fire crackles, stories swirl,
Uncle Joe's tales give our heads a whirl.
A cat leaps, knocking down the snacks,
Laughter erupts, despite the cracks.

Aunt Sally's sweater, oh what a sight,
Knitting gone wild, it's a true delight.
She claims it's fashion, we can't ignore,
It looks like a monster walked through the door.

A game of charades, a holiday gaffe,
Dad's dance moves make everyone laugh.
With each wild gesture, the room starts to cheer,
Even the Grinch would shed a tear.

As snowflakes drift and lights start to glow,
We cherish these moments; we love them so!
Gathered together, our hearts all align,
In this cozy chaos, everything's fine.

Joyful Reflections in Each Ornament

Each ornament hangs with a laugh and a tale,
That one's a winner, the rest seem to fail.
We reminisce over each clumsy craft,
When Grandma's glue turned joy into draft.

Remember the reindeer that fell off the tree?
Timmy's wild leap; oh, what a spree!
With mismatched socks and tinsel in hair,
Our holiday spirit can't help but flare.

We toast with cocoa, mugs all a-clink,
The dog steals a cookie; oh, what do you think?
A trial and error with laughter so bright,
As we tell stories through each sparkling light.

Memories linger, wrapped tight around,
In this jolly mess, we have truly found,
Christmas is more than the perfect display,
It's the goofy moments that make our day.

Winter's Embrace on Tender Hearts

Snowflakes stage a soft ballet,
While we haggle over which game to play.
Mom's stuffing burns, but don't let it go,
Dad's secret recipe was just for show.

Through frosty windows, children will cheer,
Snowball fights start, we'll conquer our fear.
Bitterly cold, yet kinship so sweet,
Until the snow is stuck to our feet!

Our mismatched mittens, a colorful flop,
As we stumble and giggle, we can't seem to stop.
Grandpa's old stories make time disappear,
They're funny, though half of them we might fear.

So gather around, let's craft joyful cheer,
With laughter our treasure, we hold so dear.
Through silly antics and warmth from the heart,
Every moment we share is a true work of art.

Singing Carols of Long Ago

Singing carols off-key, what a delight,
Our "angels" are more like a curious sight.
With mismatched hats and old flannel wear,
We make quite the duo—truly unaware.

Remember the time, we sang on the street?
The mailman joined in, it was quite a feat!
A cat stole the show, with a leap and a flip,
Our musical magic was soon on a trip.

As we laugh and we sing 'bout the trees and the snow,
A burst of nostalgia for days long ago.
Chilly fingers wrapped around a warm cup,
In this festive chaos, we're all lifted up.

So here's to the memories made with glee,
In off-tune caroling, together we're free.
Each note and each laugh, forever will flow,
Through the heartstrings of life, our melodies grow.

The Scent of Pine

The tree is up, it's all a mess,
I swear it twitched, I must confess.
Tinsel fights with all the lights,
As popcorn strands throw silly sights.

Grandma's cookies, oh so grand,
Who knew she'd burn them by a hand?
With every crumb, our laughter grows,
Her secret's out; it's recipe woes.

Uncle Joe wears socks so bold,
One green, one red, a sight to behold.
He claims it's style, we all just grin,
His fashion sense, a holiday win!

So gather 'round and raise a cheer,
For all the quirks that make us dear.
Amidst the wreaths and silly signs,
We cherish each laugh through whiffs of pines.

Flurries of Familiarity

Outside it snows, a fluffy scene,
But inside, chaos reigns supreme.
The dog's in sweaters, oh so proud,
Eating wrapping paper, feeling loud.

The kids build forts, with pillows stacked,
Pinecone missiles all intact.
They launch a volley, giggles flow,
While dad finds peace beneath the snow.

A snowman leans, his head askew,
With sunglasses on and carrot stew.
We argue still, who's best at roles,
While snowflakes dance in winter's strolls.

So let it snow, let laughter fly,
In family ties, we reach the sky.
Through flurries of glee, we find our way,
In quirks and mishaps, we laugh and sway.

Chasing Chilly Breezes

We dash outside, oh what a thrill,
Snowballs fly, it's quite the skill.
A rogue one hits my aunt in the face,
Her shout echoes, we quicken our pace.

The sleds come out, a bumpy ride,
A mix of laughter, and some pride.
But oh, that tree! It blocks our scope,
We sail right by, wish us some hope!

Hot cocoa waits with marshmallows high,
But first, we'll race 'neath the winter sky.
With goofy grins and cheeks all red,
New stories form, while joy's widespread.

As chilly breezes embrace our face,
We scoff at cold with every trace.
Amongst the snow, our hearts do sing,
With each cheeky laugh, the cheer they bring.

Fireside Tales

Gathered 'round with mugs in hand,
We spin old tales, just as we planned.
The cat's on fire, in the stories we weave,
A mythical beast, you won't believe!

Uncle's tales take wild flights,
From ghostly trips to fabulous heights.
We nod along, though half of it's spun,
His stories make us laugh and run.

Grandpa claims he once caught a star,
But it burned out quick, he didn't go far.
With every spill and playful jest,
Our fireside fun is simply the best.

So here we are, with hearts so light,
In cozy vibes that feel just right.
With every laugh that fills the air,
We paint our lives with love and care.

Rustic Roasts and Revelry

In the kitchen, chaos reigns,
Turkey's dancing, gravy's in chains.
Grandma's recipe, a mystery swirl,
We laugh so hard, it gives us a whirl.

A cousin sneezes, and pies take flight,
A fruitcake lands with a surprising bite.
Kids are giggling, they start a food fight,
And somewhere, the cat's taking off into the night.

Lights are twinkling, the tree's askew,
Someone's found eggnog, with a hazy view.
Uncle Joe's stories are all quite the same,
But we roll our eyes; it's part of the game.

Around the table, our hearts beat loud,
Laughter ripples, we're all so proud.
With every bite, we feast and rejoice,
In silly moments, we find our voice.

The Magic of Now

Snowflakes tumble, a beautiful sight,
We throw on our scarves, ready for a fight.
With snowballs flying, laughter fills the air,
We tumble and roll, without a care.

A reindeer costume? Oh dear, what a sight,
Timmy's booked it, full of pure fright.
With every mishap, we chuckle and cheer,
In the chaos of now, all's perfectly clear.

Cards are sent to relatives afar,
But did we write them? Not a single star.
Yet here we gather, no need for display,
Just silly stories and games that we play.

Music's blaring, we dance with no shame,
Even the dog has joined in the game.
In this moment, the joy it will grow,
With laughter and hugs, the true magic flows.

Layers of Love

Gift wrap's tangled; oh what a sight,
Tape is stuck while scissors take flight.
Yet as we wrestle with wrapping galore,
We burst into giggles, then tackle some more.

A secret Santa? Who bought me this sock?
It's part of a joke that truly will rock.
With every layer, surprises unfold,
Memories wrapped in ribbons of gold.

In the pile of chaos, the laughter runs high,
Between silly wishes and heartfelt sighs.
The cookies are burnt, and we start a new batch,
But we don't mind, it's all quite the catch.

So here's to the moments that cause us to grin,
The layers of love where all fun begins.
We may not be perfect, or have it all right,
But together we shine, our spirits so bright.

A Tapestry of Time

A quilt of stories, stitched up with care,
In every corner, there's laughter to share.
Grandpa's old sweater, a curious fit,
When he wore it last, we all have to admit.

With every detail, a chuckle arises,
The mishaps of years, they come as surprises.
Lost presents, tangled lights, such quite a tale,
Yet somehow, through it all, we shall prevail.

Feasting on treats from ages long past,
A fruitcake that's sturdy; it's built to last.
We raise our glasses, cheer loud and clear,
For the tapestry woven with love and with cheer.

With stories remembered, we're forever entwined,
In the fabric of time, we're joyfully aligned.
Through laughter and mishaps, together we climb,
Celebrating each moment, a bright paradigm.

Cherished Glimpses of Yesteryears

In a box of tinsel and cheer,
Old cards and ornaments appear.
Grandpa dressed as Santa, oh my!
With a potato for a pie.

Mom's fruitcake, a timeless delight,
But its texture gave us a fright.
We laughed till we dropped on the floor,
Then ate it all, begging for more.

A cat in a tree, what a scene,
With baubles flying, oh so keen!
After they've scattered, mom would shout,
"Who let the critters all roam about?"

Snowball fights and mittens in pairs,
Hot cocoa spills, and wild stares.
We reminisce, giggling so loud,
As we recall how we were proud.

A Wonderland of Remembered Smiles

A snowman lost half of his head,
An ill-timed thump when he said,
"I'll stand guard and keep out the cold!"
But he melted in sunshine, so bold.

Singing carols, oh what a tune,
Found our voices, a glorious ruin.
Off-key notes, our neighbors would fret,
But who could be mad? We had no regret.

Cookies that looked like reindeer pranced,
With sprinkles that seemed to have danced.
One bite and laughter filled the room,
What was that shape? A mix-up of doom!

The tree's lights flickered, a grand show,
Twinkling brighter, putting on glow.
The dog thought it was a new game,
Chasing shadows, oh what a fame!

Candlelight Reveries

Candle flames flickered with glee,
As we tried to make hot toddy.
But dad spilled it all, oh what a splash,
Now the floor shines with a bright flash.

A sock with a hole, a sight to see,
In the stocking, 'twas meant for me.
Santa must've been in a rush,
To miss the stitching's final hush.

Grandma's wisdom, piecing it right,
"Never wear red with stripes at night."
We giggled and later we sported,
The wildest looks she never imported.

Mirth and laughter filled the air,
As we juggled gifts without care.
Christmas moments, slightly askew,
In our hearts, they'll always feel new.

Echoes of Yesteryear

Remembering the year of the feast,
When a raccoon became our uninvited beast.
He snatched the turkey, oh what a chase,
We laughed till it hurt, embracing the grace.

Silly sweaters worn with great pride,
With reindeer dancing side by side.
A family photo captured the fun,
With mismatched outfits, we're all one!

Hot cider spills and giggles galore,
Mom's secret recipe, we always ignore.
What we think is humor, she just grins,
While we plot for our next holiday wins.

Each memory wrapped in love so bright,
In every mishap, we find the light.
Echoes ringing through laughter and cheer,
Cherishing moments that draw us near.

Tinsel Threads of Time

Once tangled lights brought endless cheer,
A cat in the tree, oh dear!
With popcorn strings and sticky hands,
We danced like reindeer in the bands.

Grandma's cookies, crisp and sweet,
She'd pinch us hard, then say, "You're neat!"
We'd hide the gifts, a sneaky feat,
And search all day, oh what a treat!

Frosty windows, silly faces,
We raced outside in mismatched laces.
Snowball fights with shrieks of glee,
The winner got to sip hot tea!

So here's to cheer and laughter loud,
With every hug, we stand so proud.
These memory threads we tightly weave,
In every heart, they never leave.

Handwritten Letters to the Past

Dear Santa, I hope you're well,
Remember that year? The Christmas spell!
You missed my list, left socks instead,
I still wear them, with pride, it's said.

Mom's fruitcake, oh what a sight,
It bounced right back with all its might!
We laughed until our stomachs hurt,
While plotting how to sneak dessert.

Uncle Joe with his Santa beard,
His ho-ho-ho seemed slightly weird.
He tripped on lights, went for a fall,
We couldn't help but burst at all!

So here's my note, a giggle or two,
Thank you for joy, and mischief too!
I'll cherish the moments, the silly fun,
In every letter, our hearts are one.

Snowflakes on Forgotten Laughs

Falling flakes, like laughter's end,
We made snowmen round the bend.
A carrot nose? Oh what a plan!
Till it melted on Uncle Stan.

Hot cocoa spills, a race to sip,
Marshmallow battles at every trip.
With sticky hands and powdered nose,
We'd dream of snow forts where joy grows.

Each winter evening, stories spun,
Of reindeer games and Christmas fun.
We'd giggle loud, then fade to dreams,
While winter whispered, or so it seems.

So let us dance in snowflakes light,
Recalling moments that feel so right.
Through all the cheer and playful scoff,
These forgotten laughs, we'll never scoff.

Nostalgic Nights Under Starlit Skies

Under the tree, we hid with glee,
Whispers of wishes, just you and me.
A knock on the door, who's it to be?
Santa or a neighbor's pet, oh what a spree!

With paper hats and silly tunes,
We danced along to the silly boons.
The clock struck twelve, oh what a fright,
We stayed up long past midnight's light.

Remember the time you tripped and fell?
We couldn't help but laugh so well.
With blankets piled and a game in hand,
The joy we share, oh isn't it grand?

So gather 'round, let stories unwind,
In every chuckle, a treasure we find.
Here's to the nights we'll never forget,
With stars above, our hearts are set.

Starlit Reflections

Twinkling lights on the tree, oh how they glow,
Mismatched socks, oh where did they go?
Cookies stuck to the roof of my mouth,
Santa's on the roof, and he's heading south!

Grandma's fruitcake, a hefty old brick,
Uncles arguing if it's a gift or a trick.
Snowball fights with dad, he slips on the path,
Laughing so hard, I forgot what I hath!

Recalled all the mishaps we had through the years,
Like Auntie's hat flying and dad's frozen tears.
Every little moment now makes us grin,
With gifts and a whole lot of laughter to spin!

So here's to the holidays, silly and bright,
With memories cherished, that stretch through the night.
Let's toast with warm cocoa, so sweet and so dear,
To the joy of the season, and friends bringing cheer!

Voices of the Past

Echoes of laughter from my childhood days,
Overcooked turkey, and Aunt Bea's wild ways.
Pine needles stuck in my hair, oh what a sight,
Giggles and snorts late into the night!

Tales from old folks, some truth, some a fib,
Like cousin Ed's dog that once swallowed a rib.
The lights flicker out as we sing off-key,
Yet every off-note is pure harmony!

Snowmen crafted with faces that melt,
Grumbling about sweaters, oh how they felt!
The smell of hot chocolate wafts through the air,
As we reminisce how we once had no care.

Loud cheers for the games that never went right,
Knocking down ornaments, oh what a fright.
So let's toast to the past, with a wink and a cheer,
For the voices that echo so vividly here!

Sledding into Memory Lane

Sledding down hills with a whoop and a shout,
Spinning and tumbling, we laughed all about.
The snowball fight led to one epic war,
While mom sipped her tea, her eyes rolling for sure!

Face-first in snow, an issue so grand,
Cousins all laughing, unable to stand.
The sledge built for two, but it's way too small,
Hilarious crash, we just can't help but fall!

Frostbite on fingers, hot cocoa so near,
Sharing wild stories, we couldn't help but cheer.
As elves in the kitchen bake pies with a flair,
The metrics of chaos—oh, they truly compare!

So here's to the joy that the season bestows,
Like snowflakes falling—each one uniquely glows.
These moments we treasure, oh can't you just see?
That sledding brings back such fond history!

Shadows of the Season

In the gloom of the night, with shadows so bended,
Broke a bauble, oh how it was ended!
Dad's dance with the broom, a sight that we loved,
As laughter erupted from the skies above!

Twinkling lights swaying, a clumsy old game,
Mom tripped on trimmings, we all felt the shame.
Uncle Joe's jokes, a whirlwind of cheer,
Though half of them came with a side of a sneer!

Whispers of yams, the burnt crispy kind,
Recipes lost in the chaos of mind.
Misplacing the gifts, so predictable—why?
But hope springs eternal when the eggnog runs dry!

So as we gather, hold dear every laugh,
Each fumble and blunder makes a beautiful path.
For in shadows of laughter, we find what we miss,
Those memories brightened with a holiday bliss!

Heartstrings and Holly

Beneath the mistletoe we stood,
Uncle Joe forgot the good food.
He tried to bake a ginger bread,
But ended up with something dead.

Laughter echoes in the halls,
Silly hats and jingle bells call.
Crazy sweaters all too bright,
Fighting over who has the best sight.

The cat finds comfort in the tree,
A festive spot, or so it believes.
With baubles hanging like fragile dreams,
It's now a toy, or so it seems.

Cookies left out in a hurry,
Santa comes, no time to worry.
He takes a bite, then shakes his head,
And leaves a note - "I'm gluten-free instead!"

When Time Stood Still

Remember when we dressed up the pup?
Ribbons and bows, oh what a setup!
He ran away, a hilarious sight,
Chasing squirrels in pure delight.

The tree stood tall, a dazzling glow,
But with one crash, all joy hit low.
Ornaments flew as the dog dashed by,
And we laughed so hard we nearly cried.

Grandma's eggnog was a strong blend,
And she kept pouring, it was hard to pretend.
She danced like a queen, so full of cheer,
We hoped her two left feet would disappear.

Snow turned to mud when the kids all came,
"Snowball fights!" they shouted, oh what a game.
In the end we soaked, all drenched with joy,
And laughed at the chaos that plagues every boy.

Soft Whispers of Winter

Whispers of snowflakes fall so slow,
Yet the kids run wild, what a show!
Building snowmen with lopsided heads,
But they aren't fierce, just silly spreads.

Our pajamas are bright, with reindeer and more,
Somehow they're stuck at the local store.
"Who wore it best?" becomes the debate,
As we pose, giggling, it feels like fate.

Sledding adventures down the street,
Until someone lands on their feet.
Mom's hot chocolate is a gooey delight,
She adds some marshmallows, yes, that's just right.

The fire crackles, we roast our treats,
Forget about worries, life's little feats.
Cousins argue over who's the best chef,
While we munch on leftovers, proof of our heft.

The Glow of Yule

Candles glowing with flickering light,
Mom's apple pie, oh, such a sight!
We make a toast with fizzy juice,
Toasting a year that's been mostly goose.

The pets wear antlers, they look so proud,
Trying to blend in with the family crowd.
They steal the show, and well, the treats,
Catching crumbs from our festive feats.

Dancing around with a mix of glee,
Twirling and whirling, let's spill some tea!
Granddad's old stories, we roll our eyes,
But in our hearts, we cherish the lies.

In this chaos, magic does unfold,
Winter tales worth more than gold.
With laughter ringing, the memories blend,
We promise again, this joy will not end.

Cocoa-Kissed Remembrances

A mug of cocoa, piled high with cream,
Marshmallows floating, it's a sweet dream.
Grandpa tells tales, with a wink and a grin,
While the cat's in the tree, counting all his sins.

Snowmen stacked high, but one lost his nose,
The dog ate it up, now he's in the prose.
We laugh and we giggle, with hearts full of cheer,
As auntie busts out her infamous reindeer.

The lights twinkle bright, like stars pure and true,
But the tinsel's a battle, conquered by the cat too.
With laughter and joy, we feast on those pies,
The echoes of giggles are the best Christmas prize.

So here's to the moments of joy and delight,
With cocoa and friends, everything feels right.
We'll cherish these days, the funny and sweet,
In the heart of the season, oh what a treat.

Evergreen Heartstrings

The tree's decorated with odd little things,
Toilet paper garlands, how laughter it brings.
With twinkling lights blinking like disco at night,
Aunt Sue in the corner is too merry to fight.

Uncle Joe's dancing, the cat leaps away,
He thinks he's a pro in this festive ballet.
Each ornament tells a peculiar old tale,
Of last year's mishaps that never grow stale.

We gather 'round feasts of cookies and cheer,
But find every plate is just crumbs, oh dear!
With faces gaudy from icing so sweet,
We giggle through bites, oh, this love is a treat.

So raise a glass high to our quirks and our charm,
To moments when mischief keeps us safe from harm.
With evergreen heartstrings and laughter in play,
We weave a fine tapestry, year after year stays.

Lanterns Flicker with Echoes

Lanterns aglow, flickering bright,
In the attic of memories, they twinkle tonight.
Grandma sings carols, a tune that's a hoot,
It sounds like a rooster in search of its route.

On the porch, we hang socks, all mismatched, it seems,
Wishing for gifts like we're living in dreams.
But all that we find is a lump on the floor,
Looks like bumbling Santa forgot once more!

The cookies go missing, each year it's the same,
The dog's wearing reindeer horns—oh, what a game!
With laughter and love sprouting strong from our hearts,
These moments unwrapped are the best kind of arts.

So let's keep the lanterns all brightly aglow,
While we dance 'round the room, with a dash of true show.
The echoes of joy will ring through the night,
And with daily mischief, our spirits take flight.

Mistletoe Dreams Beneath the Hearth

Mistletoe dangling, a critter's delight,
Uncle Tom puckers, it's quite a silly sight.
With giggles and grins, we all gather near,
Expecting some magic, yet laughter is clear.

There's a pot on the fire, a stew far too bold,
A sprinkle of chaos, or so I've been told.
We dive into food with a clatter and clang,
While Aunt Mary insists, "Just taste the dang sang!"

Outside, the snowflakes join in on the mess,
Fluffy white piles mean a day full of stress.
We roll in the cold, with our cheeks nice and red,
While stories of chaos dance 'round in our head.

So here's to the laughter, the fun and the play,
To hearth-side adventures that brighten our day.
With mistletoe wishes and memories that bloom,
We'll count every giggle as we light up the room.

The Heart of the Hearth

In the kitchen, cookies burn,
Mom's wine spills, 'Oh, wait your turn!'
Reindeer antlers on the dog,
As he snorts and hogs the log.

Grandma's sweater, bright and loud,
Almost outshining the crowd.
A cat in a Santa hat,
Plotting mischief, imagine that!

Uncle Joe with mistletoe,
Stumbles, falls – oh no, oh no!
Laughter echoes through the night,
'Twas a jolly, silly sight!

In our hearts, the cheer will stay,
Even if socks lead the way.
Nights like these spark joy again,
With big smiles, we'll do it ten!

Woven Wishes

Tinsel tangled in my hair,
'Tis the season, but beware!
Cookies stacked in piles so high,
I'm just hoping not to die!

The tree leans, what a show,
Its lights flicker, put on a glow.
Pine needles on the floor abound,
It's like a forest all around!

Auntie's hat's a sight to see,
She says it's warmth, I just say, 'Flee!'
Amidst the laughter and the cheer,
I'll find the pie, now that's sincere!

A toast to family, oh so bright,
With every blooper, pure delight.
Through the fun, we find our way,
Blessed are those who choose to stay!

Pastel Hues of the Holidays

Snowflakes fall in shades of pink,
While kids complain, 'I can't even think!'
Gingerbread houses, oh what fun,
Until you bite and break your bun!

Candy canes stuck in my hair,
I won't deny I had a scare.
Friends all gather round to cheer,
As mashed potatoes disappear!

Mom's new thing? Bright neon lights,
That turn our house into blinding sights.
And every blooper fills the room,
With warm hearts in the holiday bloom!

In laughter's glow, we sing off-key,
Dancing like there's no degree.
Amidst bright hues and joyful shifts,
It's laughter here that truly lifts!

Serenity Beneath the Snow

Beneath the flakes, a truce we find,
Snowball fights, oh how unkind!
The sledding hill, my epic fall,
As everyone laughs, I stand tall.

With cocoa spills and marshmallow clouds,
We gather 'round, a chirpy crowd.
Corny jokes fly through the air,
Granny's puns, no one can bear!

A puppy wrestles with a scarf,
Dodging mittens, he's truly daft.
Tinsel and giggles mix as one,
Creating memories full of fun!

So in this season, let's embrace,
Every awkward, funny face.
Through all the quirks one thing stays,
Joy remains in silly ways!

Fireside Whispers

By the fire, the socks are lacking,
Grandpa's snoring, we're all cracking.
The cat's seen fit to steal a treat,
While Auntie spills her drink on her feet.

The chestnuts roast with quite a flair,
Uncle Joe's dance is beyond compare.
The kids are giggling, pets in tow,
As marshmallows bounce in the ember's glow.

Cousin Lucy's wearing curtains as a dress,
Her fashion choice is a hot mess,
But laughter fills this bustling space,
And joy is worn upon each face.

In these moments, silly and bright,
We hold our memories, tight and right.
With whispers shared from near and far,
These fireside tales shine like a star.

Echoes of Yuletide Joy

In the kitchen, there's such a show,
As Grandma's cookies start to flow.
With flour clouds and frosting fights,
We laugh 'til we cry on chilly nights.

The tree is lopsided, ornaments askew,
Uncle's convinced it's a grand debut.
While lights flicker with a curious spark,
The dog thinks it's a late night lark.

Snowballs fly; the carolers croon,
While Grandma hums an off-tune tune.
The echoes linger, sweet and strange,
These memories, oh! How they rearrange.

So here's a toast, with cocoa cups,
To all the fun and silly hiccups.
In every giggle and every cheer,
The spirit of the season is here!

Glistening Moments in December's Glow

Twinkling lights wrapped on the cat,
Dad trips over, oh, imagine that!
The tinsel's tangled in a great big mess,
But laughter follows, no need to stress.

Cookies crumble, chocolate galore,
While kids sneak bites and then ignore.
The smell of pine fills up the room,
As snowflakes fall, we all can bloom.

Grandpa's jokes are outdated, it's true,
But we laugh hard, that's what we do.
The fun we have is worth more than gold,
As stories are shared and memories unfold.

These moments shine bright like festive lights,
Creating warmth on the coldest nights.
We cherish the humor, love, and cheer,
In December's glow, we hold it dear.

Cinnamon and Cradle Songs

Cinnamon swirls through the kitchen air,
While Dad and the kids start a playful dare.
The pie is baking, but so is the fun,
With laughter and joy until we're done.

Auntie croons a lullaby or two,
The baby giggles, what's she gonna do?
While grandpa spins tales of Christmas past,
All the while, the snowy wind blasts.

Hot chocolate spills on Grandma's chair,
But she just laughs with love to spare.
The cloud of marshmallows floats so high,
As we clink our mugs, "Here's to the sky!"

From silly to sweet, our hearts align,
In these moments, we richly dine.
For within these walls of merriment and song,
We find where all of us belong.

Milton Keynes UK
Ingram Content Group UK Ltd.
UKHW020818141124
451205UK00012B/635

Original title:
The Warmth of Christmas Memories

Copyright © 2024 Creative Arts Management OÜ
All rights reserved.

Author: Kieran Blackwood
ISBN HARDBACK: 978-9916-94-062-4
ISBN PAPERBACK: 978-9916-94-063-1

Scribbled Wishes in the Snow

Snowflakes dancing on my nose,
I build a snowman, with big blue toes.
He wobbles and flops with a grin so wide,
Yet down he goes for a slippery slide.

Hot cocoa spills on my winter socks,
I slip on ice while walking, oh what a shock!
Laughter echoes as I tumble right,
Guess I'll stick to the warmth inside tonight!

Voices of Winter's Embrace

Carolers sing off-key by the tree,
Their voices crack like a festive decree.
Santa's sleigh got stuck in the snow,
He's shouting, 'More reindeer, let's make it go!'

Grandma's cookies are lopsided and burnt,
Yet every bite, my taste buds are spurned.
We munch and we laugh, oh what a scene,
Celebrating flavors that defy the routine!

Cradles of Childhood Cheer

Racing down the hallway, my socks a blur,
I trip and I tumble, but what's the deter?
Presents are hiding, oh where can they be?
I'll dive in the pile, just wait and see!

A game with the cat, he swats at the bow,
It's a questionable gift, but what does he know?
Amidst all the chaos and playful delight,
These shenanigans sparkle, so merry and bright!

A Tapestry of Twinkling Lights

Twinkling bulbs flash in a dazzle so loud,
I trip on the cord, what a clumsy proud!
The tree stands tall, but lopsided for sure,
O Christmas, you silly, who knew you'd allure?

Rudolph's nose blinks like a disco ball,
While Uncle Bob dances, we all start to fall.
Jingle bells ringing, and laughter ignites,
This festive fiasco is pure holiday sights!

Time-Honored Traditions

Grandma's fruitcake, dense as a brick,
We all took a bite, it made us all sick.
Uncle Joe snores loud, like a grizzly bear,
Only to wake up, with frosting in hair.

Tree covered in tinsel, a glittery mess,
We'd blame the cat when it's time to confess.
Ornaments tangled, like lights in a knot,
Dad says, "It's fine, just takes a good shot!"

Notes of Nostalgia

Singing off-key to carols so bright,
Then tripping on boots, that gave us a fright.
Pine-scented air mixed with mom's hot stew,
Made us all giggle like the joy was brand new.

Wrapping up gifts that were slightly too late,
Last year's presents? Well, they still look great!
We'd joke and we'd laugh, with our hearts full of cheer,
Unwrapping each one, like it's just disappeared.

Yesterday's Laughter

Santa got stuck in the flue, what a sight,
We pulled him out, but he gave us a fright.
With cookies all crumbled, and milk spilled about,
We laughed till our bellies were round as a bout.

Snowball fights turned into snow-tastrophes,
Sledding downhill was a total mischief.
One tumble and roll, we'd all hit the slush,
Laughter erupted, in the frosty rush.

Cloaked in Comfort

Grandpa's old sweater, three sizes too large,
He wore it with pride like he's leading a charge.
Hot cocoa spills and marshmallows afloat,
A funny mix-up like the Christmas we wrote.

Midnight snacks claimed by a sneaky raccoon,
We found him munching beneath the full moon.
Laughter erupted, as he made his escape,
With a cocoa mustache, and a sweet little shape.

Memories Wrapped in Ribbons

A box of lights with tangled strings,
A cat naps soundly, dreaming of things.
Mom's slippers go flying, it's quite the show,
As Uncle Joe dances, despite the snow.

Grandma's old eggnog sits on the shelf,
With a hint of spice, it confuses itself.
Cousins all giggle at the fruitcake surprise,
While a snowman outside wears dad's old ties.

Socks that don't match, oh what a sight,
We toast with hot cocoa, the mood feels just right.
Tickles and laughter, all around the room,
As we cherish these times, let the silly bloom.

Toasts to Togetherness

We raise our mugs in a joyful cheer,
Grandpa starts teasing, we always want to hear.
A toast for each cousin, and one for the dog,
Who's hiding their treats under the old fog.

The roast's gone rogue, on the floor it's found,
Oh, what a family! Just sit back, astound.
Silly stories are shared as we dig right in,
With Auntie's last mishap and Uncle's old grin.

Laughter erupts at the silliest tales,
Of snowball fights ending with snow-covered veils.
Cookies baked badly, but smiles remain,
Hands raised together, through joy and through pain.

Snowflake Stories

Outside it is snowing, a magical scene,
While inside we're busy with cookies and cream.
Sledding adventures, a face full of snow,
Caught on the camera, so funny to show.

Cousins are twirling, a conga-line spree,
And someone gets tangled, oh what a sight to see!
Frosty's a legend, but he drifts with the wind,
And dad learned to snowboard, now that's how it's pinned.

Among all the giggles, a story is told,
Of snowball wars fought brave, valiant, and bold.
With gifts by the fireside, both big and small,
We have our tales mixed with laughter and all.

Warm Winks of Winter

The fireplace crackles, with magical sparks,
As Grandma swoops in, yelling, "Who's stole the tarts?"
A wink and a smile from each little face,
Holding a secret, in this warm winter space.

The kids are all dressed like giant marshmallows,
Sleds flying fast while the laughter just bellows.
Mom trips on the carpet, and down goes her drink,
We all burst with giggles, hey, what do you think?

Pine needles scatter, as we deck out the tree,
In ornaments silly, matching none of we.
With cocoa in hand, that's where joy combines,
And every sweet moment like glitter just shines.

A Melody of Memories

Jingle bells clatter, a cat takes a seat,
Stuck on the tree, oh what a feat!
Granddad's still singing his off-key tune,
While grandma's lost track of the nice and the rude.

Mittens piled high, a snowball fight,
Uncle Joe's aim was not quite right.
The snowman looks worried, his hat's a bit crooked,
As we sip hot cocoa and munch on the cookied.

Coziness and Cheer

Socks on the fire, what a great place,
They're popping and cracking, we make a race.
The lights are all blinking, the dog's in a loop,
Chasing his tail, oh what a goof troop!

Ribbons of laughter, so bright in the air,
Dad trips on the garland, oh no, it's a scare!
A pie in the oven, who should we blame?
Mom said she'd bake it, it's not the same!

Emblazed in Laughter

Each gift a surprise, the wrapping is bright,
A present for me? Oh, what a delight!
But wait, it's just socks with a glittery view,
The gift that keeps giving, from Aunt Sue, it's true!

Cookies for Santa, or so I thought,
But Rudolph just ate them, now I'm left fraught.
No milk in the fridge, a glass of old tea,
This Christmas may just end in a comedy spree!

Solstice Serenades

Carols are ringing, off-key but loud,
The neighbors all laugh, they're quite the crowd.
Harold's dance moves, a little bizarre,
He'll surely be famous, in a weird way, so far!

Eggnog spills over, our favorite drink,
It could double as glue, oh what do you think?
Laughter erupts, the magic is clear,
This silly old gathering is one we hold dear.

A Warmth That Lingers

In socks mismatched, we dance with glee,
The lights that twinkle, a sight to see.
Grandma's fruitcake, oh what a treat,
Even the cat says, "This can't be beat!"

We sip hot cocoa, marshmallow fluff,
Mom's telling stories, though we've heard enough.
The dog steals a roll, to our surprise,
As we all burst out laughing, tears in our eyes.

Gathering Around the Glowing Hearth

Gathered close, with blankets thick,
Uncle Joe starts his magic trick.
With a hat and a rabbit, he's lost his mind,
The rabbit hops off — no one can find!

The fire crackles, sparks fly high,
We roast marshmallows, oh me, oh my!
S'mores are devoured, sticky and sweet,
As Dad yells, "Fire!" — it's just our feet!

Chasing Shadows of Festive Echoes

Snowmen stand tall, with smiles so wide,
But one got a pumpkin, what a bizarre ride!
Carrot noses, eyes of coal,
In the yard, a Santa with a roll!

We chase shadows, giggling, carefree,
The neighbors peek out, oh, who could it be?
It's just us kids, a mischief-filled crew,
With reindeer antics, and a sled that flew!

Gifts of Time Tied with Ribbons

With ribbon untied, the chaos begins,
We're all on a hunt — who wins?
A box labeled "Yarn" contains a rat,
A gift from Aunt Sue — no one saw that!

We unwrap the laughter, layer by layer,
Each present a puzzle, let's be a player.
As paper flies, it's a joyful mess,
A Christmas so weird, who could guess less?

Unraveled Gifts

The ribbons flew like birds in flight,
Hiding snacks, oh what a sight!
Wrapped so tight, the paper screamed,
Hope you like what I dreamed!

A box of socks, a rubber duck,
Thought I'd fill it with my luck!
I gave you sweets, you gave me chills,
With every bite, we got our thrills!

Portraits of Peace

In sweaters bright, we pose and grin,
  Next year, let's aim for the win!
Dad's beard caught in the cookie jar,
   Merry chaos, it's our bizarre!

A picture taken, faces misaligned,
   Mom's hairdo—what a find!
 Capture the night with spicy cheer,
Snapshot of laughter through the year!

Savoring Sweet Moments

Cookies stacked like towers high,
Oops! One fell, oh my, oh my!
Milk spilled like magic tricks,
Giggling kids with sticky licks!

A feast begins, but wait, what's this?
The cat stole pie, it's such pure bliss!
We laugh and munch on all that's here,
Sweet moments like this, oh dear!

Childhood Echoes

The snowballs fly, oh how they flew,
Remember when we hit Aunt Sue?
Laughter ringing in the snowy air,
As frosty flakes tangled in our hair!

With sleds that tipped and cheeks so red,
We'd race till we crashed and fell, instead!
Those echoes of giggles, a fantasy,
Hold them close, they're pure jubilee!

Snowy Embraces

Snowflakes dance like crazy crowds,
While we chase them like little kids,
With snowmen dressed in mismatched clothes,
And carrots that forget where they hid.

Hot cocoa spills on my brand new coat,
As marshmallows float like fluffy dreams,
Uncle Joe slipped on the icy path,
And fell right into mom's yarn schemes.

We sing off-key, it's a joyous sound,
Mistletoe hangs above our heads,
Nan's cookies are as hard as bricks,
Yet we eat them all, just like she said.

Amid the laughter and goofy brawls,
We cherish moments, though some are loud,
Each snowy hug and silly fall,
Leaves a smile that's winter proud.

Treasures of the Heart

A gift that's wrapped with sparkly tape,
Looks fancy but holds a plastic toy,
Granddad chuckles at our surprise,
"Best secret ever!" says our boy.

The cat leaps up, oh what a mess,
With ribbons wrapped 'round her tiny paws,
She thinks it's all a game to play,
While we shout and give her applause.

A fruitcake sits, a family curse,
With layers that could stop a car,
Yet every year, we slice a piece,
Making legends of our bizarre.

The stories shared around the tree,
Are treasures that fill our hearts with cheer,
With laughter echoing through the night,
We gather close, year after year.

Yule Legends Revisited

The elf on the shelf, he's up to tricks,
He dances on the TV with glee,
While we're convinced that he's watching us,
Is he a spy or just goofy?

Stockings stuffed with socks and sweets,
Mom's got an eye for crafty seams,
Dad forgets to take a hint,
When asked to fix those broken dreams.

We gather 'round with lights aglow,
As Grandpa nods off in his chair,
Then wakes with tales from long ago,
Of Christmas magic that fills the air.

Each legend fills our hearts with joy,
As we swap tales and share more laughs,
With each new tale, our spirits soar,
Brother takes charge of the silly crafts.

Frost-Kissed Hues

The tree is crooked—it leans to one side,
With tinsel that looks like a bird's nest,
Ornaments swinging in a wild ride,
While the angel on top gets no rest.

Chilly winds whistle through the streets,
As we try to build a snow fort high,
But all we create is a slushy mess,
Guess the snowball fight is worth a try.

Grandma's sweater is two sizes too big,
In colors that clash like a wild dream,
She loves it still—the warmth it brings,
While we try not to giggle and scream.

With mischief brewing, the night takes flight,
As we recount tales with twinkling eyes,
In these frosty hues filled with laughter,
Are the lovely moments, our greatest prize.

Mistletoe Moments

Under the mistletoe, I made my move,
Tripped on my feet, what a funny groove!
Kissed a dear aunt who wore red lipstick,
Now I sport a print that's quite the trick.

Grandpa told jokes, oh, how they did soar,
Laughed until we fell, rolling on the floor!
A cat stole the scene, with a Christmas bow,
Lurking by the snack—oh, what a show!

A Gathering of Hearts

Family around, with stories to share,
Uncle Sam's tales, a wild, wacky flair!
Sister's new dance looks like a spastic move,
We laugh till we cry, can't help but approve.

Cousins all gathered, a photo we take,
But one of us blinked—watch that funny face break!
Gifts wrapped in layers, with endless tape,
Now we're stuck in a paper-slicing escape!

Gingerbread Dreams

Baked a gingerbread house, it leaned to the side,
The roof caved in, surprised we all cried!
I took a big bite, frosting on my nose,
Santa's not the only one with the joy that he shows.

Cookies went missing, who could it be?
The dog gave a glance, as guilty as can be!
Sprinkles on his snout, icing in his fur,
Is this canine a chef? Oh, what a stir!

Cocoa and Comfort

Cocoa in hand, I warmed up my soul,
But spilled it on Grandma, oh, how I roll!
She laughed so hard, the mug in her grip,
Now she's the one with hot chocolate on her lip.

Marshmallows floating, kids on the floor,
Bouncing around like never before!
A blanket fort made, it's cozy and bright,
But where's the cocoa? Oh, what a sight!

Sledding Down Memory Lane

Snowy hills were our playground,
We raced with laughter, face full of cold.
Sleds that flew like parachutes,
Landing in piles, stories untold.

Hot cocoa spills on mom's new chair,
Marshmallow fights, giggles and cheer.
We dressed like penguins, layers galore,
With hats so big, we could barely steer.

Mittens soaked from snowball wars,
Friction burns from sledding too fast.
But who needs warmth when you've got friends,
To laugh through chilly moments amassed.

Days like these, tangled in glee,
Noses pink under twinkling lights.
Who knew sledding could feel so grand,
With memories stored in snowy heights.

Fond Embraces Wrapped in Brightness

Auntie's hugs, like marshmallows puffed,
Squeeze too tight, you can't escape.
Her perfume smells like peppermint dreams,
Wrapped up tightly, escaping the drape.

Christmas lights blink in rhythm divine,
We twirled under stars from the attic.
Grandma's cookies, burnt just a tad,
But love made all the flavors ecstatic.

Uncle Joe's dance, such a sight!
Two left feet, but he owns the floor.
His reindeer antlers fall to the ground,
Making our sides split, hearts wanting more.

In the chaos, we find our peace,
Mom's laughter floats, joyous and bright.
Wrapped in hugs, and banter so sweet,
Family felt like magic that night.

Holly and Hope in Gentle Hues

Bright ribbons wrapped around laughter,
Holly hung asking for a kiss.
Grandpa reads with a twinkle, how sweet,
Stories that promise a little bliss.

Wrapping paper, a shimmery mess,
Cats dive in with no ounce of shame.
Presents tossed like snowflakes adrift,
Who needs toys when the cat's the game?

Ballet slippers dance with delight,
A tree decorated with eco-style.
Out of the box, our dreams take flight,
We leap and spin, all dressed with a smile.

Memories twinkle like ornaments hung,
In every crackle, a chuckle hides.
While holly and color bring us together,
It's the quirks that make our joy wide.

Echoing Laughter Through Frosted Windows

Frosted panes show our antics bold,
Snowmen with noses, shriveled and small.
We posed for pictures, stuck out our tongues,
Hoping the snow wouldn't end in a brawl.

Outside the world froze in silent bliss,
While inside we ate all the treats.
Nibbled on cookies, frosting on noses,
Racing each other for seconds and feats.

Muffin disasters, flour in the air,
Mom's face a mix of love and dismay.
Fire crackles, bringing warmth so tight,
Who needs a recipe? We play! We play!

Laughter echoes through frosted frames,
Each giggle a gift, fresh and bright.
Time stands still, in this cheerful realm,
Where memories glow like the stars at night.

Family Ties and Twinkling Lights

Gather round the fabled tree,
Where chaos swirls, oh can't you see?
Uncle Joe brings "holiday cheer,"
With laughter spilling in his beer.

Aunt May's fruitcake, hard as stone,
Leaves everyone to groan and moan.
But in the corner, kids conspire,
To set the cat's tail on fire!

The lights are dim, the bulbs are bright,
Grandpa's snoring, what a sight!
While stories told take odd twists,
And we all ponder, 'Did we exist?'

Gathered close with warmth inside,
Swapped old tales we cannot hide.
As magic swirls in silly flights,
These moments glow like twinkling lights.

Keeping Christmas Close

Sneaky Santa, what a tale,
Wrapped in jokes that never fail.
Our secret stash of tasty treats,
I see you nibbling on the sweets!

With mismatched socks, we all parade,
Into the living room, unafraid.
Grandma's punch, all spicy and nice,
A potent brew; we pay the price!

The tree is wobbling side to side,
Each ornament's a sloshed ride.
As laughter dances through the air,
I swear I saw a flying chair!

With goofy hats and silly songs,
We've turned it up; we can't go wrong.
In every hug, a quirky boast,
This time of year, we love the most.

Remnants of Yuletide Joy

Beneath the lights, we gather round,
As old tunes play, a timeless sound,
And Grandma's knitted hats, mismatched,
Are what our joyous hearts have hatched.

The cookies burned, a crispy fate,
Yet still we laugh and contemplate.
Uncle Fred tried to gift us all,
A singing fish, it made us fall!

With grand tales told of Christmas past,
We share the giggles, make them last,
As secrets spill from mouths agape,
Like Grandpa's antics, what a shape!

Through all the love, and laughter's grace,
These silly moments, we embrace.
In every glimmer, laughter's near,
Our hearts ring loud with festive cheer!

Ancestral Cheer

With cousin cards that all are wrong,
We sit back, laughing all night long.
A feast so grand, who could survive?
There's turkey leg and pie, oh my!

A game of charades turns to mayhem,
As Auntie shrieks, "You'll never tame him!"
Dressed up as elves, we laugh and play,
Our family shenanigans on display.

Uncle's jokes, they never end,
As every punchline twists a bend.
With eggnog spills and jolly roars,
We keep returning for more and more.

In cozy hugs, our hearts expand,
Through silly stories, hand in hand.
With love and laughter, it is clear,
This is the season we all hold dear.

Milestones in Mirth

A cat in a hat, what a sight,
Chasing paper balls, oh what delight!
Grandma slipped on the ice with grace,
Now she's the star of our family space.

Uncle Bob's dance, quite the show,
Spilled his drink all over Joe.
We laughed until our sides would ache,
A Christmas to remember, make no mistake!

The turkey's burnt, but we don't care,
We gobble up cookies, in our chairs,
A battle of snowballs, who'll take the prize?
Laughter erupts as the snow monster lies.

With tinsel hair and a jingle bell,
We've spun around like a carousel.
In moments like these, love fills the air,
Memories knitted, beyond compare.

Silhouettes of Celebration

Tinsel stuck on the dog's tail,
He runs like the wind, a furry snail.
A mishap with lighting, oh what a scene,
We lit up the house like a bad Halloween!

Grandpa's snoring under the tree,
With a cookie stash, as happy as can be.
Sister sings off-key, what a cheer,
We hand her a mic, she's the star here!

Reindeer games that went awry,
A flying sleigh ride, nearly to the sky.
We laughed 'til we cried, can't keep track,
Of who wore the antlers, and who wore the sack.

In the warmth of the room, jokes fly around,
Echoes of laughter, the best kind of sound.
We celebrate quirks that make us whole,
In each silly moment, love's the goal.

Threads of Togetherness

Knitting sweaters far too tight,
We all look like sausages tonight!
A cheer when the cookies somehow flop,
"Let's order pizza!" — Oh, what a swap!

Grandma's putting marshmallows in stew,
We debate if that's something we'd do.
A game of charades, hilariously poor,
We act like penguins, and then roll on the floor!

In a mix of laughter, joy floods the night,
With inside jokes that feel just right.
A gift from last year, still in the wrap,
"Is this my old sweater?" it's all a trap!

With friends and family, we gather close,
Counting the blessings that matter most.
In funny mishaps, we find our cheer,
In the love we share, we hold most dear.

Whispers in the Wind

A snowman fell and rolled away,
Chasing after him was quite the play.
Our snowflakes' battle, a frosty war,
And hot cocoa spills on the kitchen floor!

There's a sock on the cat — what a funny sight,
As he struts through the room, all filled with delight.
Dad's got candy canes stuck in his beard,
"It's all part of Christmas," he proudly cheered!

Slippers on the dog, he's a merry sight,
Barking at bells that jingle all night.
We tell silly stories, and laugh 'til we cry,
As the moon shines bright in the frosty sky.

Around the table, our hearts are aglow,
With tales of mishaps in the recent snow.
Each chuckle, each grin, a gift that we lend,
In the spirit of joy, our hearts never end.

Echoes Beneath the Stars

Twinkling lights and silly hats,
We danced with dogs and sang with cats.
Grandma's fruitcake, a brick in disguise,
We laughed so hard, tears filled our eyes.

The sleigh ride went off a tiny cliff,
Santa yelled, 'Hey, where's my gift?'
Mistletoe hung way too high,
We all got stuck, oh my, oh my!

Frosty melted, oh what a shame,
He slipped on ice while playing a game.
We built him back with half a grin,
He winked at us, let the fun begin!

In memory's vault, joy holds the key,
Each goofy mishap, a gem, you see.
Under the stars, we raise a cheer,
For laughter shared, the best time of year!

The Hearthstone Haven

Gathered 'round the fire's glow,
Uncle Joe lost track of his toe.
He wore a sock that looked like this:
A reindeer's face, we couldn't miss!

Cookies vanished in a blink,
Elves must've come, we start to think.
Dad filled his eggnog, oh so bold,
Now he's dancing like he's five years old.

Watching the cat chase tinsel strings,
He thought he'd caught all the shiny things.
With each pounce and jump, our hearts would race,
Turns out he just wanted a cozy place.

The warmth of laughter fills the room,
As stories swirl like a fragrant plume.
Around the hearth, we share a grin,
Thanking fortune for the joyful din.

Flickering Firelight

In firelight's glow, the stories blend,
Of turkey mishaps and a sock that bend.
Mom's soufflé soared up to its height,
Then dropped like it lost its will to fight.

Cousin Larry in a Santa suit,
He couldn't fit through the front, oh, shoot!
We had a laugh, he wriggled away,
With sparkly lights, signs of dismay.

Hiding gifts became a grand old time,
I found a sweater that looked like a crime.
Neighbors peeked in with a curious glare,
'What's with that outfit? Just don't compare!'

Through flickering flames, memories rise,
With silly tales and starry skies.
We gather tight, our hearts in tune,
Creating magic beneath the moon.

Branches of the Past

Decking the halls with mismatched flair,
Some ornaments hung with delicate care.
Yet a cat played hide-and-seek in the tree,
Somersaults down — oh, what a spree!

The gifts were wrapped with duct tape woes,
Dad couldn't find where the ribbon goes.
A gingerbread house made of pure delight,
But someone nibbled it, oh, what a sight!

Forgotten socks in the Santa sack,
A mystery box we just can't keep track.
Labels askew, names in a spin,
We've learned by now, chaos must win.

Branching through laughter, we reminisce,
Each goofy moment, a hug we don't miss.
In every cheer that echoes near,
We hold those quirks so dear, so dear.

Stories Spun by the Fire's Glare

The fire crackles, stories swirl,
Uncle Joe's tales give our heads a whirl.
A cat leaps, knocking down the snacks,
Laughter erupts, despite the cracks.

Aunt Sally's sweater, oh what a sight,
Knitting gone wild, it's a true delight.
She claims it's fashion, we can't ignore,
It looks like a monster walked through the door.

A game of charades, a holiday gaffe,
Dad's dance moves make everyone laugh.
With each wild gesture, the room starts to cheer,
Even the Grinch would shed a tear.

As snowflakes drift and lights start to glow,
We cherish these moments; we love them so!
Gathered together, our hearts all align,
In this cozy chaos, everything's fine.

Joyful Reflections in Each Ornament

Each ornament hangs with a laugh and a tale,
That one's a winner, the rest seem to fail.
We reminisce over each clumsy craft,
When Grandma's glue turned joy into draft.

Remember the reindeer that fell off the tree?
Timmy's wild leap; oh, what a spree!
With mismatched socks and tinsel in hair,
Our holiday spirit can't help but flare.

We toast with cocoa, mugs all a-clink,
The dog steals a cookie; oh, what do you think?
A trial and error with laughter so bright,
As we tell stories through each sparkling light.

Memories linger, wrapped tight around,
In this jolly mess, we have truly found,
Christmas is more than the perfect display,
It's the goofy moments that make our day.

Winter's Embrace on Tender Hearts

Snowflakes stage a soft ballet,
While we haggle over which game to play.
Mom's stuffing burns, but don't let it go,
Dad's secret recipe was just for show.

Through frosty windows, children will cheer,
Snowball fights start, we'll conquer our fear.
Bitterly cold, yet kinship so sweet,
Until the snow is stuck to our feet!

Our mismatched mittens, a colorful flop,
As we stumble and giggle, we can't seem to stop.
Grandpa's old stories make time disappear,
They're funny, though half of them we might fear.

So gather around, let's craft joyful cheer,
With laughter our treasure, we hold so dear.
Through silly antics and warmth from the heart,
Every moment we share is a true work of art.

Singing Carols of Long Ago

Singing carols off-key, what a delight,
Our "angels" are more like a curious sight.
With mismatched hats and old flannel wear,
   We make quite the duo—truly unaware.

Remember the time, we sang on the street?
The mailman joined in, it was quite a feat!
A cat stole the show, with a leap and a flip,
   Our musical magic was soon on a trip.

As we laugh and we sing 'bout the trees and the snow,
   A burst of nostalgia for days long ago.
Chilly fingers wrapped around a warm cup,
   In this festive chaos, we're all lifted up.

So here's to the memories made with glee,
In off-tune caroling, together we're free.
Each note and each laugh, forever will flow,
Through the heartstrings of life, our melodies grow.

The Scent of Pine

The tree is up, it's all a mess,
I swear it twitched, I must confess.
Tinsel fights with all the lights,
As popcorn strands throw silly sights.

Grandma's cookies, oh so grand,
Who knew she'd burn them by a hand?
With every crumb, our laughter grows,
Her secret's out; it's recipe woes.

Uncle Joe wears socks so bold,
One green, one red, a sight to behold.
He claims it's style, we all just grin,
His fashion sense, a holiday win!

So gather 'round and raise a cheer,
For all the quirks that make us dear.
Amidst the wreaths and silly signs,
We cherish each laugh through whiffs of pines.

Flurries of Familiarity

Outside it snows, a fluffy scene,
But inside, chaos reigns supreme.
The dog's in sweaters, oh so proud,
Eating wrapping paper, feeling loud.

The kids build forts, with pillows stacked,
Pinecone missiles all intact.
They launch a volley, giggles flow,
While dad finds peace beneath the snow.

A snowman leans, his head askew,
With sunglasses on and carrot stew.
We argue still, who's best at roles,
While snowflakes dance in winter's strolls.

So let it snow, let laughter fly,
In family ties, we reach the sky.
Through flurries of glee, we find our way,
In quirks and mishaps, we laugh and sway.

Chasing Chilly Breezes

We dash outside, oh what a thrill,
Snowballs fly, it's quite the skill.
A rogue one hits my aunt in the face,
Her shout echoes, we quicken our pace.

The sleds come out, a bumpy ride,
A mix of laughter, and some pride.
But oh, that tree! It blocks our scope,
We sail right by, wish us some hope!

Hot cocoa waits with marshmallows high,
But first, we'll race 'neath the winter sky.
With goofy grins and cheeks all red,
New stories form, while joy's widespread.

As chilly breezes embrace our face,
We scoff at cold with every trace.
Amongst the snow, our hearts do sing,
With each cheeky laugh, the cheer they bring.

Fireside Tales

Gathered 'round with mugs in hand,
We spin old tales, just as we planned.
The cat's on fire, in the stories we weave,
A mythical beast, you won't believe!

Uncle's tales take wild flights,
From ghostly trips to fabulous heights.
We nod along, though half of it's spun,
His stories make us laugh and run.

Grandpa claims he once caught a star,
But it burned out quick, he didn't go far.
With every spill and playful jest,
Our fireside fun is simply the best.

So here we are, with hearts so light,
In cozy vibes that feel just right.
With every laugh that fills the air,
We paint our lives with love and care.

Rustic Roasts and Revelry

In the kitchen, chaos reigns,
Turkey's dancing, gravy's in chains.
Grandma's recipe, a mystery swirl,
We laugh so hard, it gives us a whirl.

A cousin sneezes, and pies take flight,
A fruitcake lands with a surprising bite.
Kids are giggling, they start a food fight,
And somewhere, the cat's taking off into the night.

Lights are twinkling, the tree's askew,
Someone's found eggnog, with a hazy view.
Uncle Joe's stories are all quite the same,
But we roll our eyes; it's part of the game.

Around the table, our hearts beat loud,
Laughter ripples, we're all so proud.
With every bite, we feast and rejoice,
In silly moments, we find our voice.

The Magic of Now

Snowflakes tumble, a beautiful sight,
We throw on our scarves, ready for a fight.
With snowballs flying, laughter fills the air,
We tumble and roll, without a care.

A reindeer costume? Oh dear, what a sight,
Timmy's booked it, full of pure fright.
With every mishap, we chuckle and cheer,
In the chaos of now, all's perfectly clear.

Cards are sent to relatives afar,
But did we write them? Not a single star.
Yet here we gather, no need for display,
Just silly stories and games that we play.

Music's blaring, we dance with no shame,
Even the dog has joined in the game.
In this moment, the joy it will grow,
With laughter and hugs, the true magic flows.

Layers of Love

Gift wrap's tangled; oh what a sight,
Tape is stuck while scissors take flight.
Yet as we wrestle with wrapping galore,
We burst into giggles, then tackle some more.

A secret Santa? Who bought me this sock?
It's part of a joke that truly will rock.
With every layer, surprises unfold,
Memories wrapped in ribbons of gold.

In the pile of chaos, the laughter runs high,
Between silly wishes and heartfelt sighs.
The cookies are burnt, and we start a new batch,
But we don't mind, it's all quite the catch.

So here's to the moments that cause us to grin,
The layers of love where all fun begins.
We may not be perfect, or have it all right,
But together we shine, our spirits so bright.

A Tapestry of Time

A quilt of stories, stitched up with care,
In every corner, there's laughter to share.
Grandpa's old sweater, a curious fit,
When he wore it last, we all have to admit.

With every detail, a chuckle arises,
The mishaps of years, they come as surprises.
Lost presents, tangled lights, such quite a tale,
Yet somehow, through it all, we shall prevail.

Feasting on treats from ages long past,
A fruitcake that's sturdy; it's built to last.
We raise our glasses, cheer loud and clear,
For the tapestry woven with love and with cheer.

With stories remembered, we're forever entwined,
In the fabric of time, we're joyfully aligned.
Through laughter and mishaps, together we climb,
Celebrating each moment, a bright paradigm.

Cherished Glimpses of Yesteryears

In a box of tinsel and cheer,
Old cards and ornaments appear.
Grandpa dressed as Santa, oh my!
With a potato for a pie.

Mom's fruitcake, a timeless delight,
But its texture gave us a fright.
We laughed till we dropped on the floor,
Then ate it all, begging for more.

A cat in a tree, what a scene,
With baubles flying, oh so keen!
After they've scattered, mom would shout,
"Who let the critters all roam about?"

Snowball fights and mittens in pairs,
Hot cocoa spills, and wild stares.
We reminisce, giggling so loud,
As we recall how we were proud.

A Wonderland of Remembered Smiles

A snowman lost half of his head,
An ill-timed thump when he said,
"I'll stand guard and keep out the cold!"
But he melted in sunshine, so bold.

Singing carols, oh what a tune,
Found our voices, a glorious ruin.
Off-key notes, our neighbors would fret,
But who could be mad? We had no regret.

Cookies that looked like reindeer pranced,
With sprinkles that seemed to have danced.
One bite and laughter filled the room,
What was that shape? A mix-up of doom!

The tree's lights flickered, a grand show,
Twinkling brighter, putting on glow.
The dog thought it was a new game,
Chasing shadows, oh what a fame!

Candlelight Reveries

Candle flames flickered with glee,
As we tried to make hot toddy.
But dad spilled it all, oh what a splash,
Now the floor shines with a bright flash.

A sock with a hole, a sight to see,
In the stocking, 'twas meant for me.
Santa must've been in a rush,
To miss the stitching's final hush.

Grandma's wisdom, piecing it right,
"Never wear red with stripes at night."
We giggled and later we sported,
The wildest looks she never imported.

Mirth and laughter filled the air,
As we juggled gifts without care.
Christmas moments, slightly askew,
In our hearts, they'll always feel new.

Echoes of Yesteryear

Remembering the year of the feast,
When a raccoon became our uninvited beast.
He snatched the turkey, oh what a chase,
We laughed till it hurt, embracing the grace.

Silly sweaters worn with great pride,
With reindeer dancing side by side.
A family photo captured the fun,
With mismatched outfits, we're all one!

Hot cider spills and giggles galore,
Mom's secret recipe, we always ignore.
What we think is humor, she just grins,
While we plot for our next holiday wins.

Each memory wrapped in love so bright,
In every mishap, we find the light.
Echoes ringing through laughter and cheer,
Cherishing moments that draw us near.

Tinsel Threads of Time

Once tangled lights brought endless cheer,
A cat in the tree, oh dear!
With popcorn strings and sticky hands,
We danced like reindeer in the bands.

Grandma's cookies, crisp and sweet,
She'd pinch us hard, then say, "You're neat!"
We'd hide the gifts, a sneaky feat,
And search all day, oh what a treat!

Frosty windows, silly faces,
We raced outside in mismatched laces.
Snowball fights with shrieks of glee,
The winner got to sip hot tea!

So here's to cheer and laughter loud,
With every hug, we stand so proud.
These memory threads we tightly weave,
In every heart, they never leave.

Handwritten Letters to the Past

Dear Santa, I hope you're well,
Remember that year? The Christmas spell!
You missed my list, left socks instead,
I still wear them, with pride, it's said.

Mom's fruitcake, oh what a sight,
It bounced right back with all its might!
We laughed until our stomachs hurt,
While plotting how to sneak dessert.

Uncle Joe with his Santa beard,
His ho-ho-ho seemed slightly weird.
He tripped on lights, went for a fall,
We couldn't help but burst at all!

So here's my note, a giggle or two,
Thank you for joy, and mischief too!
I'll cherish the moments, the silly fun,
In every letter, our hearts are one.

Snowflakes on Forgotten Laughs

Falling flakes, like laughter's end,
We made snowmen round the bend.
A carrot nose? Oh what a plan!
Till it melted on Uncle Stan.

Hot cocoa spills, a race to sip,
Marshmallow battles at every trip.
With sticky hands and powdered nose,
We'd dream of snow forts where joy grows.

Each winter evening, stories spun,
Of reindeer games and Christmas fun.
We'd giggle loud, then fade to dreams,
While winter whispered, or so it seems.

So let us dance in snowflakes light,
Recalling moments that feel so right.
Through all the cheer and playful scoff,
These forgotten laughs, we'll never scoff.

Nostalgic Nights Under Starlit Skies

Under the tree, we hid with glee,
Whispers of wishes, just you and me.
A knock on the door, who's it to be?
Santa or a neighbor's pet, oh what a spree!

With paper hats and silly tunes,
We danced along to the silly boons.
The clock struck twelve, oh what a fright,
We stayed up long past midnight's light.

Remember the time you tripped and fell?
We couldn't help but laugh so well.
With blankets piled and a game in hand,
The joy we share, oh isn't it grand?

So gather 'round, let stories unwind,
In every chuckle, a treasure we find.
Here's to the nights we'll never forget,
With stars above, our hearts are set.

Starlit Reflections

Twinkling lights on the tree, oh how they glow,
Mismatched socks, oh where did they go?
Cookies stuck to the roof of my mouth,
Santa's on the roof, and he's heading south!

Grandma's fruitcake, a hefty old brick,
Uncles arguing if it's a gift or a trick.
Snowball fights with dad, he slips on the path,
Laughing so hard, I forgot what I hath!

Recalled all the mishaps we had through the years,
Like Auntie's hat flying and dad's frozen tears.
Every little moment now makes us grin,
With gifts and a whole lot of laughter to spin!

So here's to the holidays, silly and bright,
With memories cherished, that stretch through the night.
Let's toast with warm cocoa, so sweet and so dear,
To the joy of the season, and friends bringing cheer!

Voices of the Past

Echoes of laughter from my childhood days,
Overcooked turkey, and Aunt Bea's wild ways.
Pine needles stuck in my hair, oh what a sight,
Giggles and snorts late into the night!

Tales from old folks, some truth, some a fib,
Like cousin Ed's dog that once swallowed a rib.
The lights flicker out as we sing off-key,
Yet every off-note is pure harmony!

Snowmen crafted with faces that melt,
Grumbling about sweaters, oh how they felt!
The smell of hot chocolate wafts through the air,
As we reminisce how we once had no care.

Loud cheers for the games that never went right,
Knocking down ornaments, oh what a fright.
So let's toast to the past, with a wink and a cheer,
For the voices that echo so vividly here!

Sledding into Memory Lane

Sledding down hills with a whoop and a shout,
Spinning and tumbling, we laughed all about.
The snowball fight led to one epic war,
While mom sipped her tea, her eyes rolling for sure!

Face-first in snow, an issue so grand,
Cousins all laughing, unable to stand.
The sledge built for two, but it's way too small,
Hilarious crash, we just can't help but fall!

Frostbite on fingers, hot cocoa so near,
Sharing wild stories, we couldn't help but cheer.
As elves in the kitchen bake pies with a flair,
The metrics of chaos—oh, they truly compare!

So here's to the joy that the season bestows,
Like snowflakes falling—each one uniquely glows.
These moments we treasure, oh can't you just see?
That sledding brings back such fond history!

Shadows of the Season

In the gloom of the night, with shadows so bended,
Broke a bauble, oh how it was ended!
Dad's dance with the broom, a sight that we loved,
As laughter erupted from the skies above!

Twinkling lights swaying, a clumsy old game,
Mom tripped on trimmings, we all felt the shame.
Uncle Joe's jokes, a whirlwind of cheer,
Though half of them came with a side of a sneer!

Whispers of yams, the burnt crispy kind,
Recipes lost in the chaos of mind.
Misplacing the gifts, so predictable—why?
But hope springs eternal when the eggnog runs dry!

So as we gather, hold dear every laugh,
Each fumble and blunder makes a beautiful path.
For in shadows of laughter, we find what we miss,
Those memories brightened with a holiday bliss!

Heartstrings and Holly

Beneath the mistletoe we stood,
Uncle Joe forgot the good food.
He tried to bake a ginger bread,
But ended up with something dead.

Laughter echoes in the halls,
Silly hats and jingle bells call.
Crazy sweaters all too bright,
Fighting over who has the best sight.

The cat finds comfort in the tree,
A festive spot, or so it believes.
With baubles hanging like fragile dreams,
It's now a toy, or so it seems.

Cookies left out in a hurry,
Santa comes, no time to worry.
He takes a bite, then shakes his head,
And leaves a note - "I'm gluten-free instead!"

When Time Stood Still

Remember when we dressed up the pup?
Ribbons and bows, oh what a setup!
He ran away, a hilarious sight,
Chasing squirrels in pure delight.

The tree stood tall, a dazzling glow,
But with one crash, all joy hit low.
Ornaments flew as the dog dashed by,
And we laughed so hard we nearly cried.

Grandma's eggnog was a strong blend,
And she kept pouring, it was hard to pretend.
She danced like a queen, so full of cheer,
We hoped her two left feet would disappear.

Snow turned to mud when the kids all came,
"Snowball fights!" they shouted, oh what a game.
In the end we soaked, all drenched with joy,
And laughed at the chaos that plagues every boy.

Soft Whispers of Winter

Whispers of snowflakes fall so slow,
Yet the kids run wild, what a show!
Building snowmen with lopsided heads,
But they aren't fierce, just silly spreads.

Our pajamas are bright, with reindeer and more,
Somehow they're stuck at the local store.
"Who wore it best?" becomes the debate,
As we pose, giggling, it feels like fate.

Sledding adventures down the street,
Until someone lands on their feet.
Mom's hot chocolate is a gooey delight,
She adds some marshmallows, yes, that's just right.

The fire crackles, we roast our treats,
Forget about worries, life's little feats.
Cousins argue over who's the best chef,
While we munch on leftovers, proof of our heft.

The Glow of Yule

Candles glowing with flickering light,
Mom's apple pie, oh, such a sight!
We make a toast with fizzy juice,
Toasting a year that's been mostly goose.

The pets wear antlers, they look so proud,
Trying to blend in with the family crowd.
They steal the show, and well, the treats,
Catching crumbs from our festive feats.

Dancing around with a mix of glee,
Twirling and whirling, let's spill some tea!
Granddad's old stories, we roll our eyes,
But in our hearts, we cherish the lies.

In this chaos, magic does unfold,
Winter tales worth more than gold.
With laughter ringing, the memories blend,
We promise again, this joy will not end.

Cocoa-Kissed Remembrances

A mug of cocoa, piled high with cream,
Marshmallows floating, it's a sweet dream.
Grandpa tells tales, with a wink and a grin,
While the cat's in the tree, counting all his sins.

Snowmen stacked high, but one lost his nose,
The dog ate it up, now he's in the prose.
We laugh and we giggle, with hearts full of cheer,
As auntie busts out her infamous reindeer.

The lights twinkle bright, like stars pure and true,
But the tinsel's a battle, conquered by the cat too.
With laughter and joy, we feast on those pies,
The echoes of giggles are the best Christmas prize.

So here's to the moments of joy and delight,
With cocoa and friends, everything feels right.
We'll cherish these days, the funny and sweet,
In the heart of the season, oh what a treat.

Evergreen Heartstrings

The tree's decorated with odd little things,
Toilet paper garlands, how laughter it brings.
With twinkling lights blinking like disco at night,
Aunt Sue in the corner is too merry to fight.

Uncle Joe's dancing, the cat leaps away,
He thinks he's a pro in this festive ballet.
Each ornament tells a peculiar old tale,
Of last year's mishaps that never grow stale.

We gather 'round feasts of cookies and cheer,
But find every plate is just crumbs, oh dear!
With faces gaudy from icing so sweet,
We giggle through bites, oh, this love is a treat.

So raise a glass high to our quirks and our charm,
To moments when mischief keeps us safe from harm.
With evergreen heartstrings and laughter in play,
We weave a fine tapestry, year after year stays.

Lanterns Flicker with Echoes

Lanterns aglow, flickering bright,
In the attic of memories, they twinkle tonight.
Grandma sings carols, a tune that's a hoot,
It sounds like a rooster in search of its route.

On the porch, we hang socks, all mismatched, it seems,
Wishing for gifts like we're living in dreams.
But all that we find is a lump on the floor,
Looks like bumbling Santa forgot once more!

The cookies go missing, each year it's the same,
The dog's wearing reindeer horns—oh, what a game!
With laughter and love sprouting strong from our hearts,
These moments unwrapped are the best kind of arts.

So let's keep the lanterns all brightly aglow,
While we dance 'round the room, with a dash of true show.
The echoes of joy will ring through the night,
And with daily mischief, our spirits take flight.

Mistletoe Dreams Beneath the Hearth

Mistletoe dangling, a critter's delight,
Uncle Tom puckers, it's quite a silly sight.
With giggles and grins, we all gather near,
Expecting some magic, yet laughter is clear.

There's a pot on the fire, a stew far too bold,
A sprinkle of chaos, or so I've been told.
We dive into food with a clatter and clang,
While Aunt Mary insists, "Just taste the dang sang!"

Outside, the snowflakes join in on the mess,
Fluffy white piles mean a day full of stress.
We roll in the cold, with our cheeks nice and red,
While stories of chaos dance 'round in our head.

So here's to the laughter, the fun and the play,
To hearth-side adventures that brighten our day.
With mistletoe wishes and memories that bloom,
We'll count every giggle as we light up the room.

The Heart of the Hearth

In the kitchen, cookies burn,
Mom's wine spills, 'Oh, wait your turn!'
Reindeer antlers on the dog,
As he snorts and hogs the log.

Grandma's sweater, bright and loud,
Almost outshining the crowd.
A cat in a Santa hat,
Plotting mischief, imagine that!

Uncle Joe with mistletoe,
Stumbles, falls – oh no, oh no!
Laughter echoes through the night,
'Twas a jolly, silly sight!

In our hearts, the cheer will stay,
Even if socks lead the way.
Nights like these spark joy again,
With big smiles, we'll do it ten!

Woven Wishes

Tinsel tangled in my hair,
'Tis the season, but beware!
Cookies stacked in piles so high,
I'm just hoping not to die!

The tree leans, what a show,
Its lights flicker, put on a glow.
Pine needles on the floor abound,
It's like a forest all around!

Auntie's hat's a sight to see,
She says it's warmth, I just say, 'Flee!'
Amidst the laughter and the cheer,
I'll find the pie, now that's sincere!

A toast to family, oh so bright,
With every blooper, pure delight.
Through the fun, we find our way,
Blessed are those who choose to stay!

Pastel Hues of the Holidays

Snowflakes fall in shades of pink,
While kids complain, 'I can't even think!'
Gingerbread houses, oh what fun,
Until you bite and break your bun!

Candy canes stuck in my hair,
I won't deny I had a scare.
Friends all gather round to cheer,
As mashed potatoes disappear!

Mom's new thing? Bright neon lights,
That turn our house into blinding sights.
And every blooper fills the room,
With warm hearts in the holiday bloom!

In laughter's glow, we sing off-key,
Dancing like there's no degree.
Amidst bright hues and joyful shifts,
It's laughter here that truly lifts!

Serenity Beneath the Snow

Beneath the flakes, a truce we find,
Snowball fights, oh how unkind!
The sledding hill, my epic fall,
As everyone laughs, I stand tall.

With cocoa spills and marshmallow clouds,
We gather 'round, a chirpy crowd.
Corny jokes fly through the air,
Granny's puns, no one can bear!

A puppy wrestles with a scarf,
Dodging mittens, he's truly daft.
Tinsel and giggles mix as one,
Creating memories full of fun!

So in this season, let's embrace,
Every awkward, funny face.
Through all the quirks one thing stays,
Joy remains in silly ways!

Fireside Whispers

By the fire, the socks are lacking,
Grandpa's snoring, we're all cracking.
The cat's seen fit to steal a treat,
While Auntie spills her drink on her feet.

The chestnuts roast with quite a flair,
Uncle Joe's dance is beyond compare.
The kids are giggling, pets in tow,
As marshmallows bounce in the ember's glow.

Cousin Lucy's wearing curtains as a dress,
Her fashion choice is a hot mess,
But laughter fills this bustling space,
And joy is worn upon each face.

In these moments, silly and bright,
We hold our memories, tight and right.
With whispers shared from near and far,
These fireside tales shine like a star.

Echoes of Yuletide Joy

In the kitchen, there's such a show,
As Grandma's cookies start to flow.
With flour clouds and frosting fights,
We laugh 'til we cry on chilly nights.

The tree is lopsided, ornaments askew,
Uncle's convinced it's a grand debut.
While lights flicker with a curious spark,
The dog thinks it's a late night lark.

Snowballs fly; the carolers croon,
While Grandma hums an off-tune tune.
The echoes linger, sweet and strange,
These memories, oh! How they rearrange.

So here's a toast, with cocoa cups,
To all the fun and silly hiccups.
In every giggle and every cheer,
The spirit of the season is here!

Glistening Moments in December's Glow

Twinkling lights wrapped on the cat,
Dad trips over, oh, imagine that!
The tinsel's tangled in a great big mess,
But laughter follows, no need to stress.

Cookies crumble, chocolate galore,
While kids sneak bites and then ignore.
The smell of pine fills up the room,
As snowflakes fall, we all can bloom.

Grandpa's jokes are outdated, it's true,
But we laugh hard, that's what we do.
The fun we have is worth more than gold,
As stories are shared and memories unfold.

These moments shine bright like festive lights,
Creating warmth on the coldest nights.
We cherish the humor, love, and cheer,
In December's glow, we hold it dear.

Cinnamon and Cradle Songs

Cinnamon swirls through the kitchen air,
While Dad and the kids start a playful dare.
The pie is baking, but so is the fun,
With laughter and joy until we're done.

Auntie croons a lullaby or two,
The baby giggles, what's she gonna do?
While grandpa spins tales of Christmas past,
All the while, the snowy wind blasts.

Hot chocolate spills on Grandma's chair,
But she just laughs with love to spare.
The cloud of marshmallows floats so high,
As we clink our mugs, "Here's to the sky!"

From silly to sweet, our hearts align,
In these moments, we richly dine.
For within these walls of merriment and song,
We find where all of us belong.

Milton Keynes UK
Ingram Content Group UK Ltd.
UKHW020818141124
451205UK00012B/635

9 789916 940631